M·E·N·U · M·A·S·T·E·R·S

ENTERTAINING

EDITED BY
RHONA NEWMAN

OCTOPUS BOOKS

MENU-MATCH CODE
To allow more flexibility within the menus we have added
bold numbers after certain recipes to offer suitable
alternatives.
Thus, if the numbers ·3·11·14· appear after a starter, they
indicate that the starter of Menu 3, 11, or 14 could be
substituted.
Using the MENU-MATCH CODE you will be sure to find
a menu to suit all tastes.

NOTES
Standard spoon measurements are used in all recipes
1 tablespoon = one 15 ml spoon
1 teaspoon = one 5 ml spoon
All spoon measures are level
Where amounts of salt and pepper are not specified, the
cook should use her own discretion.
Canned foods should not be drained, unless so stated in the
recipe. For all recipes, quantities are given in metric,
imperial and American measures. Follow one set of
measures only, because they are not interchangeable.

Jacket photograph:
Noisettes of Lamb,
Raspberry and Hazelnut Roll.

First published 1986 by
Octopus Books Limited
59 Grosvenor Street, London W1

© 1986 Octopus Books Limited

ISBN 0 7064 2540 5

Produced by Mandarin Publishers Ltd
22a Westlands Rd
Quarry Bay, Hong Kong
Printed in Hong Kong

C · O · N · T · E · N · T · S

I·N·T·R·O·D·U·C·T·I·O·N

Planning a large and lavish celebration? Throwing a party? Or simply having family and friends round for a summer gathering? Do not be daunted by the prospect, or stuck for ideas. Menu Masters 'Entertaining' will inspire even the most reluctant cook towards effortless entertaining with a range of delicious new menus for all manner of occasions.

The most successful parties are always the result of good forward planning. Whether it is a portable picnic or a relaxed dinner for two, a good host or hostess will always be armed with indispensable preparation notes and lists. A well-chosen menu, the right setting ingredients and a detailed time-plan enable you to relax and enjoy your party equally as much as your guests. Menu Masters 'Entertaining' does all this preparation for you, so taking the worry and effort out of giving parties. Menus have been carefully selected to balance colour, taste and texture in a mouth-watering combination of dishes. The introduction to each menu gives useful hints and tips on entertaining and offers advice on suitable wines. The detailed countdowns allow you to prepare as much as possible in advance, with the option to make full use of the freezer if you have one. A final time-plan will then take you step by step to serving and make sure everything arrives at the table on time.

Throughout the book helpful labour-saving advice, rescue tactics for possible disasters and suggestions for recipe variations make sure you have all the information necessary to produce the perfect meal. Use the menu-match numbers at the end of the recipes to create your own combinations and add even more sumptuous meals to your repertoire.

M · E · N · U

· 1 ·

Nice 'n' Easy for 4

Chicken Walnut Parcels
Buttered Celeriac
Runner Beans with Carrots

·

Shortbread Biscuits
Rhubarb Brûlée

What better way to spend an evening with friends than over a casual, relaxed supper at home? This kind of meal can be arranged at the last minute as you may well have a chicken, beans and rhubarb in the freezer. Chicken flavourings and the shortbread ingredients can probably be found in the store cupboard, so it would only be necessary to shop for the carrots, celeriac and soured (sour) cream.

An elaborate dessert is not essential for this meal: a brûlée is very easy to prepare and particularly delicious if it is thoroughly chilled before placing under the grill (broiler), providing a contrast of chilled fruit and the hot caramelized sugar on top.

Informal Settings

This simple menu can be served either at lunchtime or in the early evening. On a winter evening it could be served around the fire on trays. If a table is set, it would be quite acceptable to serve it in a cosy kitchen or family area rather than in a formal dining room.

A light Anjou rosé or a white Muscadet would be suitable or you may prefer to serve cider or beer for this nice 'n' easy meal.

Make sure you chill the drinks well before serving.

Chicken Walnut Parcels

Metric/Imperial	American
50 g/2 oz butter	¼ cup butter
1 onion, chopped	1 onion, chopped
1 teaspoon paprika	1 teaspoon paprika
50 g/2 oz walnuts, chopped	½ cup chopped walnuts
½ teaspoon finely grated orange rind	½ teaspoon finely grated orange rind

salt	salt
freshly ground black pepper	freshly ground black pepper
4 chicken pieces	1 broiler, cut up
To Garnish:	For Garnish:
1 tablespoon chopped fresh parsley or 1 tablespoon chopped fresh basil	1 tablespoon chopped fresh parsley or 1 tablespoon chopped fresh basil
orange slices or twists	orange slices or twists

1. Melt the butter in a small saucepan and sauté the onion until soft. Add the paprika and cook for 1 minute. Remove from the heat and stir in the walnuts and orange rind.

2. Sprinkle the chicken pieces with salt and pepper and place each on a square of foil large enough to wrap the portion completely.

3. Divide the onion mixture between the chicken pieces, then fold over the foil to make well-sealed parcels.

4. Place on a baking sheet and cook in a preheated oven (190°C/375°F), Gas Mark 5, for about 40 minutes or until the chicken is tender.

5. Transfer the chicken to a warm serving dish and pour the juices from the parcels over the top. Garnish with parsley and orange slices or twists. Serve with jacket baked potatoes.

Buttered Celeriac

Metric/Imperial	American
750 g/1 ½ lb celeriac, leaves and root fibres removed	1 ½ lb celeriac, leaves and root fibers removed
25 g/1 oz butter	2 tablespoons butter
salt	salt
freshly ground black pepper	freshly ground black pepper
chopped fresh parsley or chives, to garnish	chopped fresh parsley or chives, for garnish

1. Wash the celeriac and cut into large pieces.

2. Cook in a saucepan of boiling salted water for about 1 hour or until just tender. Test with a skewer after 45 minutes.

3. Drain, peel and slice. Toss in butter and add salt and pepper to taste. Garnish with chopped parsley or chives. Serve immediately.
(Alternatively, cook the celeriac until very soft. Drain and purée with the butter and seasoning.)

Chicken walnut parcels

Runner Beans with Carrots

Metric/Imperial	American
250 g/8 oz young carrots, sliced	½ lb young carrots, sliced
salt	salt
freshly ground black pepper	freshly ground black pepper
500 g/1 lb runner beans, thinly sliced	3 cups thinly sliced green beans
2 tablespoons oil	2 tablespoons oil
½ teaspoon dried thyme	½ teaspoon dried thyme

1. Put the carrots in a saucepan of water. Add salt and pepper to taste, cover and cook for 10 minutes.

2. Add the beans and oil. Sprinkle with the thyme. Cover and cook for a further 10 minutes, then drain.

3. Transfer to a warm serving dish. ·4·

Shortbread Biscuits

Metric/Imperial	American
175 g/6 oz plain flour	1 ½ cups all-purpose flour
good pinch of salt	good pinch of salt
125 g/4 oz butter, softened	½ cup softened butter
40 g/1 ½ oz caster sugar	3 tablespoons superfine sugar
extra sugar, for sprinkling	extra sugar, for sprinkling

1. Sift the flour and salt into a bowl. Add the butter and sugar and mix with a wooden spoon. Knead the mixture into a ball. Turn on to a lightly floured surface and shape into a round.

2. Flour a rolling pin and roll out the mixture to about 1 cm/½ inch thick. Using a 6 cm/2½ inch fluted cutter, cut into rounds and place on a baking sheet.

3. Sprinkle lightly with sugar and cook in a preheated oven (160°C/325°F), Gas Mark 3, for about 15 to 20 minutes or until pale golden. Leave for 1 to 2 minutes before easing off with a palette knife. Place on a wire rack to cool. Makes 12 to 16.

Rhubarb Brûlée

Metric/Imperial	American
500 g/1 lb rhubarb, chopped	1 lb rhubarb, chopped
2 teaspoons water	2 teaspoons water
½ teaspoon ground cinnamon	½ teaspoon ground cinnamon
50 g/2 oz granulated sugar	¼ cup sugar
150 ml/¼ pint soured cream	⅔ cup sour cream
soft brown sugar	light brown sugar

1. Place the rhubarb in a saucepan with the water, cinnamon and sugar. Cook gently until soft.
2. Divide the fruit between four flameproof ramekin dishes. Spoon the soured (sour) cream over the top. Cover and chill until required.
3. Sprinkle liberally with brown sugar. Place under a preheated moderate grill (broiler) until the sugar caramelizes.
4. Serve immediately or chill again before serving.

Cook's Tip:
If soured (sour) cream is not available, single (light) cream can be soured with 1 teaspoon lemon juice. Alternatively use half single (light) cream and half plain (unflavored) yogurt.

C · O · U · N · T · D · O · W · N

The day before:
Defrost the chicken if using frozen. Stew the rhubarb, cover and store in the refrigerator. Make the shortbread, cool and store in an airtight container.

On the day:
Make up the Chicken Walnut Parcels, place on a baking sheet and refrigerate. Prepare the carrots and leave in cold water. Prepare the beans and place in a polythene (plastic) bag in the refrigerator. Chop the parsley or chives for garnish and refrigerate. Assemble the brûlées without the sugar, cover and chill in the refrigerator.

To serve at 7.30 pm:
6.00: Set the table or lay out on trays requirements for a fireside meal. Prepare the celeriac, cover with cold water and lemon juice to prevent discoloration.
6.30: Chill the white wine or lager. Preheat the oven. Cook the celeriac.
6.45: Place the chicken parcels in the oven. Prepare the orange and parsley garnish. Cover and refrigerate until required.
7.00: Place the shortbread on a plate and sprinkle with a little caster (superfine) sugar.
7.10: Cook the carrots.
7.20: Add the beans, oil and thyme.
7.30: Transfer the chicken to a serving dish and garnish. Slice the celeriac. Toss in butter and season. Dish up the vegetables.

Sprinkle the brown sugar over the brûlées just before placing under the grill (broiler).

F · R · E · E · Z · E · R · N · O · T · E · S

The Chicken Walnut Parcels can be frozen. Drain off any excess liquid and freeze separately. Cool the parcels and place the foil wrappings in a freezer bag and seal. Thaw the parcels and excess liquid in the refrigerator overnight and combine the two when reheated. The shortbread can also be frozen. Pack in a rigid container and seal. Thaw at room temperature for 3 to 4 hours.

Cook's Tip:
'Parcels' are a quick, simple and colourful way to serve pieces of meat or fish for small numbers. They can be prepared ahead and kept in the refrigerator until ready to cook. Serve them straight onto heated serving plates for each diner to open his or her own parcel.

If liked, serve with jacket-baked potatoes or hot garlic bread (see page 20) cooked in the oven at the same time. Wrap the potatoes or garlic bread in foil for the guest to unwrap with the chicken parcels. Serve with extra sour cream, plain (unflavored) yogurt) or butter.

═M·E·N·U═

· 2 ·

Make-ahead Meal for 4

Cream of Watercress Soup
·
Burgundy Beef with Olives
Glazed Carrots and 'Nips
Gratin Dauphinois
·
Pear and Orange Tart

If you lead a busy life or are out at work all day and feel that there is never time to entertain, then a plan-ahead meal is the answer. Decide on your menu, then during a weekend, or a couple of evenings before the meal, set aside time to prepare some of the food.

Freezer Standbys

Obviously, a freezer is ideal for advance preparation. Soup is always a useful starter as it freezes well. Reduce the liquid in the Cream of Watercress Soup by omitting the milk until after thawing.

Any form of casserole is ideal for making ahead. The Burgundy Beef with Olives can be frozen or made 1 or 2 days ahead and stored in the refrigerator. This ensures that the flavours really have time to develop.

A mixture of root vegetables makes a good accompaniment to the beef. Although the dish cannot be frozen, the vegetables can be prepared, blanched and frozen.

Pear and Orange Tart makes an interesting dessert to complete the meal. It can be made well in advance and frozen. Serve cold or warm.

A medium red Burgundy is ideal to serve with this hearty meal.

Cream of Watercress Soup

Metric/Imperial	American
50 g/2 oz butter	1/4 cup butter
1 onion, sliced	1 onion, sliced
2 bunches watercress, washed, roughly chopped	2 bunches watercress, washed, roughly chopped
450 ml/3/4 pint chicken stock	2 cups chicken stock
25 g/1 oz flour	1/4 cup flour
300 ml/1/2 pint milk	1 1/4 cups milk
salt	salt
freshly ground black pepper	freshly ground black pepper
1 tablespoon cream	1 tablespoon cream
To Garnish:	For Garnish:
watercress	watercress
croûtons (optional)	croûtons (optional)

1. Melt half the butter in a saucepan and sauté the onion until soft. Stir in the watercress and cook for a further few minutes. Pour in the stock, cover and simmer for 20 minutes. Allow to cool slightly.

2. Melt the remaining butter in another pan and stir in the flour. Cook for 1 minute, stirring, and remove from the heat.

3. Gradually stir in the milk then return to the heat and bring to the boil, stirring all the time. Pour into the watercress and stock.

4. Cool slightly, then transfer to a blender or food processor and blend to a smooth cream. Taste and add salt and pepper to taste.

5. Return to the pan and heat through. Stir in the cream and transfer to warm soup bowls. Garnish with watercress and croûtons, if using. ·3·8·

Cook's tip:

The Burgundy Beef with Olives can be cooked in the oven. Place in a flameproof casserole dish, and bring to the boil. Cover tightly and cook in a preheated oven (180°C/350°F), Gas Mark 4, for 1 1/2 to 2 hours or until tender.

Burgundy Beef with Olives

Metric/Imperial	American
750 g/1 1/2 lb beef topside, in 1 piece	1 1/2 lb piece round roast rump beef
2 tablespoons plain flour	2 tablespoons all-purpose flour
salt	salt
freshly ground black pepper	freshly ground black pepper
12 black olives, stoned	12 pitted ripe olives
12 blanched and skinned almonds	12 blanched and skinned almonds
2 tablespoons vegetable oil	2 tablespoons vegetable oil
15 g/1/2 oz butter	1 tablespoon butter
1 large onion, sliced	1 large onion, sliced
250 g/8 oz back bacon, derinded and chopped	1/2 lb Canadian bacon, derinded and chopped
1 bay leaf	1 bay leaf
300 ml/1/2 pint Burgundy	1 1/4 cups Burgundy
chopped fresh parsley, to garnish	chopped fresh parsley, for garnish

1. Cut the beef into 12 pieces, each about 5 cm/2 inches square. Toss in the flour, seasoned with salt and pepper, until evenly coated.

2. Stuff each olive with an almond. Make a small hole in the centre of each piece of beef, then push a stuffed olive into each hole. Press the beef together again to hold the olives.

3. Heat the oil and butter in a large flameproof casserole and sauté the onion for 5 minutes without browning.

4. Add the beef and brown well on all sides. Add the bacon and bay leaf. Cook, stirring for a further 1 to 2 minutes. Stir in the wine.

5. Bring to the boil, then lower the heat, cover and simmer for 1 1/2 hours or until the beef is tender. Discard the bay leaf. Garnish with parsley just before serving.

Gratin dauphinois

Glazed Carrots and 'Nips

Metric/Imperial	American
750 g/1 1/2 lb mixed carrots, turnips and parsnips	1 1/2 lb mixed carrots, turnips and parsnips
50 g/2 oz butter	1/4 cup butter
1 teaspoon soft brown sugar	1 teaspoon soft brown sugar
2 teaspoons Worcestershire sauce	2 teaspoons Worcestershire sauce
salt	salt
freshly ground black pepper	freshly ground black pepper
fresh parsley, to garnish	fresh parsley, for garnish

1. Cut the vegetables into thin strips about 6 cm/ 2 1/2 inches long. Cook in a saucepan of boiling salted water until just tender. Drain and keep warm.
2. Melt the butter in a pan and stir in the sugar, Worcestershire sauce, salt and pepper.
3. Add the vegetables and toss until well coated. Transfer to a warm serving dish and garnish. ·1·

Gratin Dauphinois

Metric/Imperial	American
750 g/1 1/2 lb floury potatoes, peeled and sliced	1 1/2 lb floury potatoes, peeled and sliced
25 g/1 oz butter	2 tablespoons butter
1-2 cloves garlic, peeled and halved	1-2 cloves garlic, peeled and halved
200 ml/1/3 pint milk	7/8 cup milk
6 tablespoons single cream	6 tablespoons light cream
1/2 teaspoon salt	1/2 teaspoon salt
freshly ground black pepper	freshly ground black pepper
grated nutmeg	grated nutmeg

1. Lightly grease a shallow flameproof casserole dish and cover the base with potato slices to a depth of about 2.5-4 cm/1-1 1/2 inches; the dish will look attractive if you overlap the slices.
2. Melt the butter in a pan and sauté the garlic until golden brown. Pour over the potatoes.

3. Meanwhile, heat the milk and cream in a pan. Add the salt, pepper and nutmeg to taste and pour over the potatoes.

4. Cover the dish with foil and cook in a preheated oven (190°C/375°F), Gas Mark 5, for 45 minutes or until the potatoes are cooked.

5. Just before serving, remove the foil and place the dish under a preheated grill (broiler) until the top is brown.

Pear and Orange Tart

Metric/Imperial	American
rich shortcrust pastry, made with 250 g/8 oz plain flour, 175 g/6 oz fat, and 2-3 tablespoons cold water	rich pie crust dough made with 2 cups all-purpose flour, ¾ cup fat and 2-3 tablespoons cold water
1 × 411 g/14½ oz can pear halves, drained	1 × 15 oz can pear halves, drained
finely grated rind and juice of ½ orange	finely grated rind and juice of ½ orange
egg white, beaten, for glazing	egg white, beaten, for glazing
caster sugar, for sprinkling	sugar, for sprinkling
150 ml/¼ pint whipping cream, to finish	⅔ cup whipping cream, to finish

1. Roll out half the pastry (dough) and use to line a 20 cm/8 inch plain flan ring. Prick the base with a fork then arrange the pear halves in the ring. Sprinkle with the orange rind and juice.

2. Roll out the remaining pastry to make a lid. Using a 7.5 cm/3 inch plain cutter, make a cut-out circle in the centre. Carefully lift the pastry and place over the pears. Seal the edges well.

3. Brush with egg white and sprinkle with sugar. Cook in a preheated oven (190°C/375°F), Gas Mark 5, for about 35 minutes or until the tart is golden.

4. Allow to cool, then remove the tart from the flan ring and place on a serving plate.

5. Lightly whip the cream and spoon or pipe some into the central space of the tart. Serve the remainder separately. ·4·5·

C·O·U·N·T·D·O·W·N

Two days before:
Make up the Burgundy Beef with Olives. Cook, cool and store in the refrigerator for 1 to 2 days. Make up the Pear and Orange Tart, cool, cover and store in the refrigerator or airtight container for up to 2 days.

The day before:
Make the soup, without the cream, and store in the refrigerator. Prepare the root vegetables and place in cold water in the refrigerator or in a sealed polythene (plastic) bag. Make up the Gratin Dauphinois to the end of stage 3. Cool, cover and refrigerate.

On the day:
Whip the cream, cover and chill. Prepare the watercress garnish; chop the parsley.

To serve at 8 pm:
6.00: Open the red wine. Prepare the table.
7.00: Preheat the oven.
7.15: Place the beef in a casserole dish and reheat in the oven. Cook the Gratin Dauphinois.
7.30: Make croûtons if serving and keep warm in the oven.
7.35: Cook the carrots, turnips and parsnips, then drain.
7.50: Reheat the soup and stir in the cream.
7.55: Preheat the grill (broiler). Prepare the glaze and toss the vegetables in it. Place in a serving dish and keep warm.
8.00: Place the Gratin Dauphinois under the grill (broiler) until brown then return to the oven to keep warm. Lower the oven temperature while taking the soup course as the food is only being kept warm. Garnish the dishes before taking to the table. Add the cream to the tart.

F·R·E·E·Z·E·R · N·O·T·E·S

See Freezer Standbys (page 9)

M·E·N·U

· 3 ·

Warming Winter Supper for 6

Crudités and Mustard Dip
·
Cassoulet
Cabbage and Walnut Salad
Baked Herb Tomatoes
·
Apple and Raisin Jalousie

A cold, dark winter evening is the best time to entertain friends cosily at home. As this is a fairly informal meal, the first course can be served sitting around the fire should you be lucky enough to have one! Side plates and napkins can be offered so that guests can take a selection of crudités and a spoonful of the dip. The hearty main course and dessert can then be served sitting at the table.

Traditional Dish

Cassoulet is an old French peasant recipe which is fairly rich and sustaining. There are many variations on the recipe but beans and pork are always included: this recipe is quite a simple version. Whenever possible this Cassoulet should be made in advance and frozen or stored in the refrigerator for 1 to 2 days to allow flavours to develop – a great advantage for the busy cook.

Apples are delicious in any form of dessert, but the Apple and Raisin Jalousie tastes and looks particularly impressive.

A good Claret would be appropriate with this menu, and a warm, spicy Glühwein served before the meal as a special aperitif. Glühwein should be made at least 2 hours before serving to allow the flavours to develop.

Crudités and Mustard Dip

Cassoulet

Crudités:

We have adopted the habit of serving raw vegetables as an hors d'oeuvre from the French. Many vegetables can be included, but they should be prepared in such a way that they are easy to eat with the fingers. Include cauliflower, young courgettes (zucchini), cucumber, fennel root, green and red peppers, radishes, spring onions (scallions) and tomatoes. You could add apples or pears. Prepare 500 g/1 lb to 750 g/1½ lb in total.

Metric/Imperial	American
2 egg yolks	2 egg yolks
1 tablespoon Dijon mustard	1 tablespoon Dijon mustard
salt	salt
freshly ground black pepper	freshly ground black pepper
1 teaspoon lemon juice	1 teaspoon lemon juice
300 ml/½ pint olive oil	1¼ cups olive oil
1 tablespoon boiling water	1 tablespoon boiling water
2 spring onions, finely chopped, to garnish	2 scallions, finely chopped, for garnish

1. Be sure that all the ingredients are at room temperature. Stir together the egg yolks, mustard and salt and pepper to taste. Stir in the lemon juice. Beat the mixture until well blended. Alternatively place the ingredients in a blender or food processor.
2. Pour on the oil drop by drop, beating all the time or working the blender or processor continuously. As the sauce thickens, pour the oil in a thin, steady stream, still beating or blending constantly. This must be done slowly to avoid curdling the mayonnaise.
3. Add the boiling water. Taste and adjust the seasoning. Spoon into a bowl, cover and chill until required. Sprinkle with the chopped spring onions (scallions) just before serving.
4. Arrange the crudités neatly on a platter and place the mustard dip in the centre. Cover and chill again before serving. ·9·

Metric/Imperial	American
1 tablespoon oil	1 tablespoon oil
1 large onion, sliced	1 large onion, sliced
125 g/4 oz bacon, chopped	¼ lb fatty bacon slices, chopped
1 kg/2 lb belly pork, cubed	2 lb fresh pork sides, cubed
125 g/4 oz dried butter beans, soaked overnight	⅔ cup dried lima beans, soaked overnight
250 g/8 oz garlic sausage, cubed	½ lb garlic sausage, cubed
750 ml/1¼ pints stock	3 cups stock
1 × 227 g/8 oz can tomatoes	1 × 8 oz can tomatoes
bouquet garni	bouquet garni
salt	salt
freshly ground black pepper	freshly ground black pepper
75 g/3 oz fresh breadcrumbs	1½ cups soft bread crumbs

1. Heat the oil in a pan and sauté the onion and bacon for 3 minutes. Add the pork and continue to cook for 5 minutes, turning the meat to brown evenly.
2. Drain the beans and add to the pan with the garlic sausage, stock, tomatoes with their juice, bouquet garni and salt and pepper to taste. Bring to the boil, stirring, and boil for 10 minutes.
3. Transfer to a 2.25 litre/4 pint (2½ quart) casserole dish. Cover and cook in a preheated oven (160°C/325°F), Gas Mark 3, for 1½ hours.
4. Remove the bouquet garni, taste and adjust the seasoning. Sprinkle with the breadcrumbs and return to the oven, uncovered, for another hour. Serve hot with baked jacket potatoes.

Variation:

Haricot (navy) beans can be used in place of butter (dried lima) beans in the Cassoulet. These should be soaked overnight, drained, covered with cold water, brought to the boil and cooked for 30 minutes. Drain and use as butter beans in the recipe.

Apple and raisin jalousie

Cabbage and Walnut Salad

Metric/Imperial	American
¼ small white cabbage, finely shredded	¼ small Dutch cabbage, finely shredded
¼ small red cabbage, finely shredded	¼ small red hard cabbage, finely shredded
1 small onion, finely chopped	1 small onion, finely chopped
2 tablespoons chopped walnuts	2 tablespoons chopped walnuts
finely grated rind and juice of 1 orange	finely grated rind and juice of 1 orange
5 tablespoons olive oil	5 tablespoons olive oil
1 teaspoon caraway seeds	1 teaspoon caraway seeds
salt	salt
freshly ground black pepper	freshly ground black pepper

1. Put the white and red cabbage into a bowl with the onion and nuts.
2. Mix the orange rind and juice with the olive oil, caraway seeds and salt and pepper to taste.
3. Stir the orange dressing into the prepared vegetables and mix well. Transfer to a serving bowl and leave to stand for 1 to 2 hours. ·1·

Baked Herb Tomatoes

Metric/Imperial	American
6 large tomatoes	6 large tomatoes
salt	salt
freshly ground black pepper	freshly ground black pepper
1 tablespoon chopped fresh basil	1 tablespoon chopped fresh basil
15 g/½ oz butter	1 tablespoon butter
watercress, to garnish	watercress, for garnish

1. Cut a fairly deep cross in the top of each tomato, open out and sprinkle with salt and pepper to taste. Divide the basil between the tomatoes.
2. Place on a grill (broiler) tray covered with foil and dot with the butter. Cook under a preheated hot grill for 4 to 5 minutes.
3. Alternatively, place in a lightly oiled ovenproof dish and cook in a preheated oven (200°C/400°F), Gas Mark 6, for 15 minutes or until the tomatoes are soft. Pierce with a skewer to test.
4. Transfer to a warm serving dish and garnish with the watercress. If not serving immediately keep warm covered loosely with foil.

Apple and Raisin Jalousie

Metric/Imperial	American
500 g/1 lb cooking apples	*1 lb tart apples*
125 g/4 oz raisins	*3/4 cup raisins*
125 g/4 oz caster sugar	*1/2 cup sugar*
1/2 teaspoon vanilla essence	*1/2 teaspoon vanilla*
1 × 375 g/13 oz packet	*1 × 13 oz pack frozen puff*
frozen puff pastry,	*dough, thawed*
thawed	*beaten egg, to glaze*
beaten egg, to glaze	*sifted confectioners' sugar,*
sifted icing sugar, to finish	*to finish*
custard, cream or plain	*custard, cream or*
yogurt, to serve	*unflavored yogurt, to*
	serve

1. Peel, core and thinly slice the apples. Mix in a bowl with the raisins, sugar and vanilla.
2. Roll out the pastry (dough) to a 35 cm/14 inch square. Cut in half, then fold one piece in half lengthways. Cut through the pastry from the folded edge to within 2.5 cm/1 inch of the cut edge, at 2.5 cm/1 inch intervals.
3. Arrange the apple and raisin mixture over the uncut piece of pastry. Place on a wetted baking sheet. Brush the edges with beaten egg. Place the cut piece of pastry over half the apple mixture. Carefully open out the pastry and press the edges to seal.
4. Pinch the edges of the pastry between the fingers and thumb all around to seal and decorate. Brush with beaten egg. Bake in a preheated oven (220°C/425°F), Gas Mark 7, for 25 to 30 minutes or until the pastry is crisp and golden.
5. Transfer to a wire rack and sprinkle with sifted icing (confectioners') sugar. Serve warm or cold with custard, cream or plain (unflavored) yogurt. ·9·

C · O · U · N · T · D · O · W · N
A few days before:
Prepare the breadcrumbs and store in the refrigerator.

The day before:
Make the Cassoulet to the end of stage 3, cool, cover and store in the refrigerator. Make up the Mustard Dip, cover and refrigerate. Make the orange dressing for the Cabbage and Caraway Salad; store in a screw-top jar. Make the Apple and Raisin Jalousie, cover and store in the refrigerator.

On the day:
Prepare the Crudités and place in a bowl of water in the refrigerator. During the afternoon, prepare the Cabbage and Walnut Salad, cover and leave at room temperature. Prepare the Baked Herb Tomatoes, place in a dish and refrigerate.

To serve at 8 pm:
6.00: Open the red wine. Make gluwein if serving. Prepare the table.
6.30: Remove the Mustard Dip from the refrigerator. Prepare the watercress garnish for the tomatoes.
6.40: Preheat the oven.
7.00: Sprinkle the breadcrumbs over the Cassoulet and place, uncovered, in the oven.
7.30: Prepare the custard, cream or yogurt to accompany the jalousie.
7.45: Drain the crudités and arrange on a platter with the dip. Cover and chill.
7.50: Line the grill (broiler) tray with foil and preheat. If serving the jalousie hot, place in the oven to warm through. Dust with icing (confectioners') sugar before serving.
7.55: Cook the tomatoes under the grill (broiler). Place on a serving dish and keep warm.
8.00: Serve the Crudités and Mustard Dip.

F · R · E · E · Z · E · R · N · O · T · E · S
Make the Cassoulet to the end of stage 3, cool, cover and freeze. Freeze for up to 3 months: thaw in the refrigerator overnight. Reheat as in stage 4 of the recipe. Prepare the breadcrumbs and freeze: thaw at room temperature. Wrap and freeze the Apple and Raisin Jalousie. Reheat from frozen at (190°C/375°F), Gas Mark 5, for 20 to 30 minutes.

MENU

· 4 ·

Simply Vegetarian for 4

Courgette Gratin
Tomato, Onion and Chive Salad
Spinach with Mint and Yogurt Dressing
Piquant Okra

Crunchy Apricot Pudding

The day you have to entertain vegetarians, panic can easily set in — what *do* they eat? Fortunately, most will eat eggs, cheese and milk products which gives scope for many dishes, and this simple menu with two hot savoury dishes and two salads is just the answer.

A Satisfying Meal

The gratin has an interesting texture and flavour, and the okra, also known as lady's fingers, makes a delightful dish with an added hint of ginger. Spinach is served here as a crisp salad; young tender leaves are delicious with the refreshing yogurt and mint dressing.

The Crunchy Apricot Pudding is a tasty wholefood dessert which uses bread in cubes rather than crumbs. Serve it hot with yogurt or ice cream. As most vegetarians will eat cheese, a cheeseboard can be offered with a selection of crackers and fruit.

Informal Settings

Attractive place mats and earthenware pottery would create a suitably simple setting for this vegetarian meal. A Chianti would go well with these dishes; or a Soave.

Courgette gratin

Courgette Gratin

Metric/Imperial	American
2 large aubergines, cut into large cubes	2 large eggplants, cut into large cubes
salt	salt
3 tomatoes, sliced	3 tomatoes, sliced
2 courgettes, sliced	2 zucchini, sliced
1 bunch of mixed herbs (e.g. parsley, basil, rosemary), chopped	1 bunch of mixed herbs (e.g. parsley, basil, rosemary), chopped
150 ml/¼ pint double cream	⅔ cup heavy cream
2 eggs, beaten	2 eggs, beaten
freshly ground black pepper	freshly ground black pepper
50 g/2 oz butter	¼ cup butter
1 clove garlic, peeled	1 clove garlic, peeled
125 g/4 oz dry white breadcrumbs	1 cup dry white bread crumbs
extra chopped fresh herbs, to garnish	extra chopped fresh herbs, for garnish

1. Sprinkle the aubergines (eggplants) with salt and leave to drain for about 15 minutes. Rinse well with cold water to remove excess salt and wipe dry with absorbent kitchen paper.
2. Arrange alternate layers of aubergine, tomato and courgette (zucchini) in a greased ovenproof dish. Sprinkle with the chopped herbs.
3. Mix the cream with the eggs, add salt and pepper to taste and pour over the vegetable mixture.
4. Melt the butter in a small pan and sauté the garlic until golden brown. Remove and discard the garlic. Add the breadcrumbs to the garlic-flavoured butter

and cook for 1 to 2 minutes.

5. Sprinkle over the vegetables in the dish. Cook in a preheated oven (180°C/350°F), Gas Mark 4, for 30 to 40 minutes or until golden brown. Serve immediately sprinkled with extra chopped fresh herbs.

Tomato, Onion and Chive Salad

Metric/Imperial	American
salt	salt
freshly ground black pepper	freshly ground black pepper
pinch dry English mustard	pinch dry English mustard
2 tablespoons olive or corn oil	2 tablespoons olive or corn oil
2 teaspoons wine vinegar	2 teaspoons wine vinegar
2 medium onions, sliced	2 medium onions, sliced
6 firm tomatoes, skinned and thinly sliced	6 firm tomatoes, skinned and thinly sliced
2 teaspoons chopped chives	2 teaspoons chopped chives

1. Make a French dressing by mixing together the salt, pepper, mustard, oil and vinegar.

2. Lay onions on a tray, sprinkle liberally with salt and leave for 30 minutes. Drain and rinse with cold water.

3. Alternate tomato slices with onion rings in a serving dish. Add the chopped chives to the French dressing and spoon over the vegetables.

Spinach with Mint and Yogurt Dressing

Metric/Imperial	American
500 g/1 lb young spinach leaves, well washed and dried	1 lb young spinach leaves, well washed and dried
4 tablespoons plain yogurt	4 tablespoons unflavored yogurt
½ teaspoon lemon juice	½ teaspoon lemon juice
salt	salt
freshly ground black pepper	freshly ground black pepper
4 teaspoons chopped fresh mint	4 teaspoons chopped fresh mint

1. Tear the spinach into pieces and put into a serving bowl.

2. Mix the yogurt with the lemon juice and add salt and pepper to taste. Stir in the chopped mint.

3. Trickle the yogurt dressing over the salad just before serving. ·6·7·

Piquant Okra

Metric/Imperial	American
350 g/12 oz okra	¾ lb okra
150 ml/¼ pint dry white wine	⅔ cup dry white wine
2 bay leaves	2 bay leaves
1 × 227 g/8 oz can tomatoes	1 × 8 oz can tomatoes
pinch of sugar	pinch of sugar
pinch of ground ginger	pinch of ground ginger
salt	salt
freshly ground black pepper	freshly ground black pepper
15 g/½ oz butter	1 tablespoon butter
1 tablespoon chopped fresh parsley	1 tablespoon chopped fresh parsley

1. Place the okra in a saucepan with the white wine and bay leaves. Bring to the boil, lower the heat and cook gently for about 8 minutes. The okra should be just tender and retain some bite.

2. Add the tomatoes with a little of their juice, the sugar, ginger and salt and pepper to taste. Stir well and cook for a further 5 minutes or until the liquid is reduced by half.

3. Add the butter and parsley, stirring well. Remove the bay leaves and transfer to a warm serving dish. Serve immediately.

Crunchy Apricot Pudding

Metric/Imperial	American
2 × 410 g/15 oz cans apricot halves	2 × 16 oz cans apricot halves
125 g/4 oz margarine	½ cup margarine
1 teaspoon ground cinnamon	1 teaspoon ground cinnamon
½ teaspoon grated nutmeg	½ teaspoon grated nutmeg
6 tablespoons clear honey	6 tablespoons runny honey
6 slices wholemeal bread	6 slices wholewheat bread
50 g/2 oz Bran Flakes breakfast cereal	2 cups Bran Flakes breakfast cereal

1. Drain the apricot halves and reserve 150 ml/ ¼ pint (⅔ cup) of the syrup.
2. Place the margarine, spices and honey in a large saucepan and heat gently. Stir well to mix then stir in the reserved syrup. Remove from the heat.
3. Remove the crusts from the bread, toast until golden on both sides and then cut into 1 cm/½ inch cubes.
4. Add to the honey mixture with the Bran Flakes and the apricot halves. Pour into a 1.5 litre/2½ pint (6 cup) ovenproof dish. Bake in a preheated oven (180°C/350°F), Gas Mark 4, for about 30 minutes. Serve hot or cold. ·2·3·

Variation:

In place of canned apricots, use 500 g/1 lb dried apricots soaked overnight. Use the liquid in place of the syrup.

C·O·U·N·T·D·O·W·N

The day before:

Make the French dressing for the Tomato, Onion and Chive Salad. Prepare the breadcrumbs and make the topping for the gratin. Cool and store in a covered container.

On the day:

Prepare the gratin, cover and refrigerate without the topping. Prepare the mint and yogurt dressing and refrigerate. Make up and cook the Crunchy Apricot Pudding. Cool, cover and refrigerate.

To serve at 8 pm:

6.00: Open the red wine. Prepare the table. Make up the cheeseboard and cover.

6.30: Salt the onions for the tomato salad. Chop the parsley for the okra.

7.00: Preheat the oven. Prepare the spinach and place in a serving bowl. Cover and chill until required.

7.15: Add the breadcrumb topping to the gratin and place in the oven.

7.25: Prepare the Tomato, Onion and Chive Salad.

7.45: Make up the Piquant Okra.

7.55: Reheat the Crunchy Apricot Pudding in the oven.

8.00: Spoon the yogurt mint dressing over the spinach. Place the okra in a warm serving dish. Take the dishes to the table.

F·R·E·E·Z·E·R·N·O·T·E·S

If freezing the gratin, cook the dish for 30 minutes, cool and cover with foil. Place in a polythene (plastic) bag, seal and freeze for up to 1 month. Thaw in the refrigerator overnight, then reheat before serving in a moderate oven for 20 to 30 minutes. Make up the Piquant Okra to the end of stage 1, and pack into a rigid container. Freeze for up to 1 month. Thaw at room temperature and continue as in the recipe. The Crunchy Apricot Pudding can be cooked, cooled and wrapped in the same way. Freeze for up to 1 month. Thaw at room temperature and serve cold or reheat in a moderate oven for 15 to 20 minutes.

Cook's Tip:

Hot French bread with garlic or herb butter could be served with this menu. It is a good idea to make up several loaves and store in the freezer. When required the bread can be reheated from frozen. One large stick will serve 6 to 8 and require 125 g/4 oz (½ cup) butter flavoured with one crushed garlic clove or 2 tablespoons of chopped mixed herbs.

MENU

· 5 ·

Family Barbecue for 8

Beefburgers
Honey Lamb Chops
Barbecue Relish
Bean and Onion Salad
·
Apple Crumble Cake

Longer summer evenings are ideal for fun barbecue parties. Any preparation can be done well in advance and everyone can share in and enjoy the cooking.

The food will taste just as good whether you use a small portable barbecue or an elaborate built-in one. For best results, the charcoal should be really hot before the food is placed on the grid. Allow the charcoal to burn for at least 30 minutes before starting to cook. Long-handled tongs are useful for turning and handling the food from a safe distance.

Quick and Simple Dishes

Burgers are a firm favourite with all ages and they are very quick and simple to make. If you have a freezer, it is worth making up large batches.

Bread and salads make the easiest accompaniments to barbecued food. The Bean and Onion Salad can be made well in advance. A green salad can also be served tossed with French dressing or a herb mayonnaise.

Refreshing Drinks

For this informal meal, lagers and cider are best. Make up large jugs of fruit juice and sparkling mineral water for those who prefer a soft drink.

Beefburgers

Metric/Imperial	American
1 kg/2 lb best minced beef	*4 cups firmly packed best*
salt	*ground beef*
freshly ground black pepper	*salt*
melted butter	*freshly ground black pepper*
8 bread baps	*melted butter*
	8 burger rolls

1. Place the beef in a bowl and mix in salt and pepper. Shape into burgers approximately 7.5 cm/ 3 inches in diameter. Stack with greaseproof (waxed) paper or cling film (plastic wrap) between each burger and chill until required.
2. Prepare the coals for a barbecue or preheat the grill (broiler). Brush both sides of each burger with melted butter and cook on the grid for 7 minutes on each side.
3. Split and toast the baps or wrap in foil and heat over the barbecue. Place the burgers in the baps and serve with relishes and/or toppings of cheese, onion slices or tomato slices.

Note:
Flavourings can also be added to the meat before making the burgers. Try one of the following: grated onion; crushed garlic; mixed herbs; curry paste.

Honey Lamb Chops

Metric/Imperial	American
8 best end lamb chops	*8 rib lamb chops*
salt	*salt*
freshly ground black pepper	*freshly ground black pepper*
50 g/2 oz butter	*¼ cup butter*
2 tablespoons honey	*2 tablespoons honey*
2 tablespoons wine vinegar	*2 tablespoons wine vinegar*
rosemary sprigs	*rosemary sprigs*
Piquant Butter, to serve	*Piquant Butter, to serve*

1. Trim the meat from the bone ends about 2.5 cm/1 inch down. Season with salt and pepper.
2. In a pan, heat the butter, honey and vinegar and use to brush over both sides of the chops.
3. Prepare the coals for a barbecue or preheat the grill (broiler). Press rosemary sprigs into the chops before placing on the grid to cook for 10 minutes on each side.
4. Serve immediately in napkins with Piquant Butter. ·6·

Piquant Butter
Soften 125 g/4 oz (½ cup) butter in a bowl and add the following:
Mint: 1½ tablespoons chopped fresh mint mixed with 2 teaspoons each of caster sugar, boiling water and vinegar. Add salt and pepper to taste.

Barbecue Relish

Metric/Imperial	American
50 g/2 oz butter	*¼ cup butter*
1 medium onion, finely	*1 medium onion, finely*
chopped	*chopped*
1 × 400 g/14 oz can	*1 × 16 oz can tomatoes*
tomatoes	*4 tablespoons chutney or*
4 tablespoons chutney	*relish*
¼ teaspoon dried marjoram	*¼ teaspoon dried marjoram*
salt	*salt*
freshly ground black pepper	*freshly ground black pepper*

1. Melt the butter in a pan and sauté the onion until soft.
2. Add the tomatoes, chutney, marjoram, salt and pepper. Heat gently until thickened. Serve chilled.

Bean and Onion Salad

Metric/Imperial	American
salt	*salt*
freshly ground black pepper	*freshly ground black pepper*
pinch dry English mustard	*pinch dry English mustard*

1 teaspoon dried basil
1 clove garlic, peeled and
    crushed
6 tablespoons olive oil
2 tablespoons wine vinegar
1 medium onion, thinly
    sliced
salt
2 × 432 g/15¼ oz cans
    red kidney beans,
    drained
chopped parsley, to garnish

1 teaspoon dried basil
1 clove garlic, peeled and
    crushed
6 tablespoons olive oil
2 tablespoons wine vinegar
1 medium onion, thinly
    sliced
salt
2 × 16 oz cans red kidney
    beans, drained
chopped parsley, for garnish

1. Make a French dressing by combining the salt, pepper, mustard, herbs, garlic, oil and vinegar in a screw-top jar.

2. Place the onion rings on a plate and sprinkle with salt. Leave for 30 minutes than drain and rinse in cold water to remove excess salt. Pat dry on absorbent kitchen paper.

3. Rinse the beans with cold water and place in a bowl. Add the onion rings and dressing, then toss well together.

4. Serve garnished with parsley.

Cook's Tip:
If at the last moment the weather is unsuitable for a barbecue, all the food can be cooked under the grill (broiler) or in the oven.

Honey lamb chops; Beefburgers; corn on the cob; Piquant butter; Barbecue relish; fresh fruit; bread rolls

Apple Crumble Cake

Metric/Imperial	American
Topping:	Topping:
75 g/3 oz self-raising flour	*¾ cup self-rising flour*
25 g/1 oz butter	*2 tablespoons butter*
25 g/1 oz caster sugar	*2 tablespoons sugar*
1 tablespoon water	*1 tablespoon water*
Base:	Base:
50 g/2 oz margarine	*¼ cup margarine*
50 g/2 oz caster sugar	*¼ cup sugar*
1 large egg, beaten	*1 large egg, beaten*
few drops vanilla essence	*few drops vanilla*
125 g/4 oz self-raising flour, sifted	*1 cup self-rising flour, sifted*
2 medium cooking apples, peeled, cored, and sliced	*2 medium tart apples, peeled, cored and sliced*
To Finish:	To Finish:
1 red eating apple, sliced	*1 red eating apple, sliced*
icing sugar	*confectioners' sugar*
whipped cream	*whipped cream*

1. Grease a 20 cm/8 inch sandwich tin (layer cake pan) and line the base with non-stick (parchment) paper.
2. To make the topping, sift the flour into a bowl and rub in (cut in) the butter until the mixture resembles fine breadcrumbs. Stir in the sugar. Sprinkle on the water and mix until the mixture becomes lumpy. Set aside.
3. To make the base, place the margarine and sugar in a bowl and cream until light and fluffy. Gradually beat in the egg and vanilla, then fold in the flour.
4. Spread the mixture over the base of the prepared tin. Arrange the apple slices on top. Sprinkle the crumble topping over the apple. Bake in a preheated oven (180°C/350°F), Gas Mark 4, for 45 minutes to 1 hour.
5. Cool slightly then remove from the tin. Decorate with apple slices, dust with icing (confectioners') sugar. Serve, cut into wedges, with whipping cream.

The day before:
Make up the burgers and wrap with paper between them. Store in the refrigerator. Make up the Barbecue Relish and place in a covered container in the refrigerator. Make the glaze for the chops and refrigerate. Make the Piquant Butter and refrigerate. Make up a French dressing and keep in a screw-top jar. If serving a green salad, make up a herb mayonnaise using fresh herbs if possible. Make the Apple Crumble Cake but don't decorate yet. Wrap and store in an airtight container.

On the day:
Prepare the lamb chops and cover with the glaze. Cover and refrigerate. Prepare the Bean and Onion Salad, cover and leave at room temperature. Prepare a green salad if serving. Decorate the Apple Crumble Cake. Cover and leave at room temperature. Whip the cream and place in the refrigerator.

To serve at 7.30 pm:
6.00: Chill any drinks. Place ice in a container and put in the freezer.
6.30: Prepare and light the barbecue. Oil the grid.
6.45: Prepare the fruits for the dip.
7.00: Set out the plates, cutlery, glasses, etc. Place the relishes, salads and bread on the table.
7.10: Place the lamb on the barbecue.
7.15: Place the Beefburgers on the barbecue.
7.20: Toast the baps. Turn the lamb chops.
7.25: Turn the Beefburgers.
7.30 approximately: Start serving the food.

F · R · E · E · Z · E · R   N · O · T · E · S
Made-up burgers can be frozen for up to 3 months. Wrap individually or with greaseproof paper or cling film (plastic wrap) between each for easy removal. These are best cooked from frozen as they hold their shape better. The Barbecue Relish can be frozen for 1 to 2 months, but the flavour may become stronger. Thaw overnight in the refrigerator.

MENU

· 6 ·

Portable Picnic for 6

Avocado and Shrimp Quiches
Devilled Drumsticks
Mushroom Salad
Mandarin Rice Salad
·
Date and Honey Cake

Summer is the time when entertaining can include picnics. The catering for any outdoor meal demands food to suit the occasion – simple to eat and easy to transport. Cold boxes and insulated bags are useful whether you are travelling a short or a long distance. There are many attractive picnic hampers to buy with all the accessories if you are regular outdoor-eaters, but any box or basket can be used. Some occasions may call for taking tables and chairs, but for most picnics a cloth on the ground with the food laid out on serving plates will be ideal. Brightly coloured paper or plastic plates are a good idea if you do not want to risk taking china ones. Also take along glasses or plastic mugs, cutlery, serving spoons, napkins and a couple of damp cloths.

Well-chilled Wines

A special picnic should include a light crisp white wine such as Frascati or Vinho Verde. This should be well chilled before leaving and carried in an insulated container. Be sure to place the wine in the container just before leaving home to ensure that it stays cool until required. Take along plenty of soft drinks and mineral water too, especially if the weather is very warm.

Avocado and Shrimp Quiches

Metric/Imperial	American
350 g/12 oz shortcrust pastry	3/4 lb basic pie dough
3 small avocados, peeled, stoned and chopped	3 small avocados, peeled, pitted and chopped
175 g/6 oz peeled shrimps	1 cup shelled shrimp
450 ml/3/4 pint single cream	2 cups light cream
6 eggs	6 eggs
salt	salt
freshly ground black pepper	freshly ground black pepper
grated Parmesan cheese, for sprinkling	grated Parmesan cheese, for sprinkling

1. Roll out the pastry (dough) and use to line 6 × 10 cm/4 inch individual loose-bottomed flan tins or 2 × 20 cm/8 inch flan tins or dishes. Pinch up the edges of the pastry well. Prick the bottom. Bake 'blind' in a preheated oven (190°C/375°F), Gas Mark 5, for 5 minutes.

2. Divide the chopped avocado and shrimps between the pastry cases (pie shells). Beat the cream with the eggs and add salt and pepper to taste. Pour into the pastry cases and sprinkle with grated Parmesan cheese.

3. Return to the oven and bake for 20 to 25 minutes or until the filling has set. Leave to cool in the tins.

Devilled Drumsticks

Metric/Imperial	American
12 chicken drumsticks	12 chicken drumsticks
2 teaspoons salt	2 tablespoons salt
2 teaspoons sugar	2 teaspoons sugar
1 teaspoon freshly ground black pepper	1 teaspoon freshly ground black pepper
1 teaspoon ground ginger	1 teaspoon ground ginger
1 teaspoon dry mustard	1 teaspoon dry mustard
50 g/2 oz butter, melted	1/4 cup melted butter
Sauce:	Sauce:
2 tablespoons tomato ketchup	2 tablespoons tomato ketchup
1 tablespoon mushroom ketchup	1 tablespoon mushroom ketchup
1 tablespoon Worcestershire sauce	1 tablespoon Worcestershire sauce
1 tablespoon soy sauce	1 tablespoon soy sauce
4 drops Tabasco sauce	4 drops hot pepper sauce
1 tablespoon plum jam	1 tablespoon plum jam

1. Score the chicken skin with a sharp knife and place in a shallow dish. In a bowl, mix together the salt, sugar, pepper, ginger and mustard powder.

2. Dust the chicken completely with this mixture and leave for 1 hour. Brush the chicken with the melted butter.

3. Mix the sauce ingredients in a saucepan and heat gently.

4. Cook the chicken drumsticks under a preheated moderate grill (broiler) for 10 to 15 minutes or until brown and crisp, basting with the hot sauce.

5. Allow to cool and pack into rigid containers. Store in the refrigerator until required. Place any remaining sauce in a covered container to serve with the chicken. ·5·

Mushroom Salad

Metric/Imperial	American
a few Chinese leaves, finely shredded	a few bok choy leaves, finely shredded
Dressing:	Dressing:
1 tablespoon mango chutney	1 tablespoon mango chutney
2 teaspoons curry paste	2 teaspoons curry paste
300 ml/1/2 pint soured cream	1 1/4 cups sour cream
2 dessert apples, peeled, cored and diced	2 eating apples, peeled, cored and diced
	salt

Date and honey cake.

salt
freshly ground black pepper
250 g/8 oz button
   mushrooms, trimmed

freshly ground black pepper
2 cups button mushrooms,
   trimmed

1. Arrange the Chinese leaves (bok choy) in a serving bowl.
2. To make the dressing, blend the chutney with the curry paste and cream.
3. Add the apple to the curry mixture together with a little salt and pepper and the mushrooms.
4. Spoon this mixture over the Chinese leaves just before serving.

Cook's Tip:
If a barbecue can be taken to the picnic, cook the chicken drumsticks on it and serve hot.

Mandarin Rice Salad

Metric/Imperial	American
250 g/8 oz long-grain rice, washed	1¼ cups long-grain rice, washed
1 × 312 g/11 oz can mandarin oranges, drained	1 × 11 oz can mandarin oranges, drained
3 spring onions, finely chopped	3 scallions, finely chopped
75 g/3 oz salted peanuts	½ cup salted peanuts
freshly ground black pepper	freshly ground black pepper
5 tablespoons French dressing	5 tablespoons French dressing

1. Cook the rice in a saucepan of boiling salted water for about 10 to 15 minutes until just tender. Drain and run cold water through the rice to separate grains. Transfer to a bowl.
2. Stir in the mandarin oranges, spring onions (scallions) and salted peanuts. Add plenty of freshly ground black pepper.
3. Stir in the French dressing and serve chilled. ·5·

Date and Honey Cake

Metric/Imperial	American
250 g/8 oz wholemeal flour	2 cups wholewheat flour
pinch of salt	pinch of salt
2 teaspoons baking powder	2 teaspoons baking powder
75 g/3 oz soft light brown sugar	½ cup soft light brown sugar
6 tablespoons clear honey	6 tablespoons runny honey
grated rind of 1 orange	grated rind of 1 orange
6 tablespoons concentrated orange juice	6 tablespoons concentrated orange juice
175 ml/6 fl oz vegetable oil	¾ cup vegetable oil
2 eggs, beaten	2 eggs, beaten
175 g/6 oz dates, stoned and finely chopped	1 cup pitted chopped dates
Topping:	Topping:
25 g/1 oz butter	2 tablespoons butter
40 g/1½ oz plain flour	6 tablespoons all-purpose flour
40 g/1½ oz demerara sugar	¼ cup raw sugar

1. Sift together the flour, salt and baking powder. Tip any bran retained in the sieve back into the flour. Mix together the sugar, honey, orange rind, orange juice and oil in a bowl. Beat in the eggs. Gradually beat in the flour mixture, then stir in the dates.
2. Turn the mixture into a greased and lined 18 cm/7 inch cake tin (cake pan) and level the top.
3. For the topping, rub (cut) the butter into the flour until crumbly. Stir in the sugar and sprinkle over the cake.

4. Bake in a preheated oven (160°C/325°F), Gas Mark 3, for 1¼ hours or until the cake is well risen and firm.
5. Leave the cake to cool a little in the tin, then transfer to a wire rack to cool completely. ·2·3·7·

C·O·U·N·T·D·O·W·N
The day before:
Make the Date and Honey Cake and store in an airtight container. Make the Avocado and Shrimp Quiches and store in the refrigerator. Cook the Devilled Drumsticks and place in the refrigerator overnight. Pack any remaining sauce into a rigid container and refrigerate. Make the Mandarin and Rice Salad. Place in a serving bowl without adding the dressing. Cover and refrigerate overnight. Make up the dressing and store in a screw-top jar.
For a lunchtime picnic:
9.30: Chill the white wine.
10.30: Pack a hamper, basket or box with all the accessories.
11.00: Prepare the Chinese leaves (bok choy), drain well and dry. Place in a polythene (plastic) bag and refrigerate. Make the mushroom and apple mixture and pack into a rigid container then refrigerate.
11.30: Add the dressing to the Mandarin Rice Salad and cover with cling film (plastic wrap).
11.40: Pack the food and wine into cold boxes.
About 12 noon: Depart.

F·R·E·E·Z·E·R·N·O·T·E·S
Cook the Avocado and Shrimp Quiches, cool and wrap in foil. Pack into polythene (plastic) bags, seal and freeze. Thaw in the refrigerator overnight or at room temperature for 4 to 6 hours. Make the Date and Honey Cake, cool and store in an airtight container for 1 day before freezing. Wrap in foil and place in a polythene (plastic) bag. Seal and freeze. Thaw in the refrigerator overnight or at room temperature for 6 to 8 hours. (Alternatively, cut into portions before freezing and thaw as required.)

MENU

· 7 ·

Summer Buffet for 12

Chicken with Seafood Sauce
Chilled Ratatouille
Watercress and Walnut Salad

·

Linzer Cream Tarts with Raspberry Sauce

A buffet-style party is the best way of entertaining more than a handful of people, and careful planning will ensure success. Even if you haven't a freezer, cold food, as in this menu, can be made up well in advance.

Setting a Buffet Table

With a fork meal no formal table setting is necessary, but the table can look just as attractive: a fresh or dried flower arrangement can form a centrepiece and, for an evening gathering, candles always create a pleasant atmosphere.

Lay the forks out at one end of the table with paper or cloth napkins, neatly folded. Plates can be stacked near the forks so that guests can help themselves. Remember to place serving spoons with each dish of food. If the table is large enough, set out the glasses and drinks on it. A dry white wine such as a Graves would accompany this menu well, but soft drinks should also be served.

Optional Extras

A bowl of fresh fruit can be placed on the table as an additional or alternative dessert. It is also a good idea to serve a simple cheeseboard of, say, a ripe piece of Brie and one of Cheddar.

E·N·T·E·R·T·A·I·N·I·N·G

Chicken with Seafood Sauce

Metric/Imperial

2 × 1.5 kg (3½ lb)
    chickens
thinly pared rind of
    2 lemons
1 large onion, thinly sliced
2 bay leaves
600 ml/1 pint dry white
    wine
chicken stock
8 anchovy fillets, chopped
24 prawns in shells
salt
freshly ground black pepper
Sauce:
4 egg yolks
juice of 1 lemon
600 ml/1 pint olive oil
freshly ground black pepper
2 tablespoons capers
2 × 200 g/7 oz cans tuna
    fish, drained
To Garnish:
2 tablespoons capers
12 anchovy fillets
lemon twists
basil sprigs

American

2 × 3½ lb chickens
thinly pared rind of
    2 lemons
1 large onion, thinly sliced
2 bay leaves
2½ cups dry white wine
chicken stock
8 anchovy fillets, chopped
24 shrimp in shells
salt
freshly ground black pepper
Sauce:
4 egg yolks
juice of 1 lemon
2½ cups olive oil
freshly ground black pepper
2 tablespoons capers
2 × 7 oz cans tuna fish,
    drained
For Garnish:
2 tablespoons capers
12 anchovy fillets
lemon twists
basil sprigs

1. Place the chickens in a large pan with the lemon rind, onion, bay leaves, white wine and sufficient stock to half cover them. Add the anchovies.
2. Peel the prawns (shrimp), cover and refrigerate. Add the shells and salt and pepper to the pan. Bring to the boil, cover and simmer for 1½ hours.
3. To make the sauce, beat the egg yolks with the lemon juice then gradually whisk in the olive oil. Place the mayonnaise sauce in a blender or food processor and add the pepper, capers and tuna fish. Blend until smooth.
4. Remove the chickens from the pan and add enough of the strained cooking liquor to the sauce to give a smooth coating consistency.
5. Carve the chickens and arrange on a serving platter. Spoon a little of the prepared sauce over the top and chill.
6. Garnish with the prawns (shrimp), capers, anchovy fillets, lemon and basil. Serve the rest of the sauce separately. ·13·

Chilled Ratatouille

Metric/Imperial

4 medium aubergines, cut
    into 1 cm/½ inch cubes
salt
12 tablespoons vegetable oil
2 medium onions, sliced
6 cloves garlic, peeled and
    crushed
4 red peppers, cored, seeded
    and sliced
2 green peppers, cored,
    seeded and sliced
750 g/1½ lb courgettes,
    sliced
500 g/1 lb tomatoes, peeled
    and chopped
250 g/8 oz button
    mushrooms, sliced
2 × 50 g/2 oz cans tomato
    purée
600 ml/1 pint hot chicken
    stock
freshly ground black pepper
2 tablespoons chopped fresh
    mint
4 tablespoons chopped fresh
    parsley

American

4 medium eggplants, cut
    into ½ inch cubes
salt
12 tablespoons vegetable oil
2 medium onions, sliced
6 cloves garlic, peeled and
    crushed
4 red peppers, cored, seeded
    and sliced
2 green peppers, cored,
    seeded and sliced
5¼ cups sliced zucchini
2 cups peeled, chopped
    tomatoes
2 cups sliced mushrooms
¼ lb tomato paste
2½ cups hot chicken stock
freshly ground black pepper
2 tablespoons chopped fresh
    mint
4 tablespoons chopped fresh
    parsley

1. Put the aubergine (eggplant) cubes into a colander and sprinkle with salt. Leave them to drain for 30 minutes. Rinse off the salt and dry the cubes on absorbent kitchen paper.

2. Heat the oil in a large pan and sauté the onion and garlic over a moderate heat for 2 minutes, stirring once or twice. Add the aubergine cubes and stir-fry for a further 2 minutes. Add the peppers and courgettes (zucchini), and fry for 3 minutes. Add the tomatoes and mushrooms and cook for 2 minutes.

3. Mix together the tomato purée (paste) and hot stock and pour over the vegetables. Season.

4. Bring to the boil, cover and simmer for 15 to 20 minutes or until the vegetables are only just tender – they should not 'collapse' and lose their shape.

5. Stir the herbs into the ratatouille. Taste and season again if necessary. Allow to cool, then chill. ·4·

Chicken with seafood sauce

Watercress and Walnut Salad

Metric/Imperial	American
2 bunches watercress	*2 bunches watercress*
1 tablespoon French mustard	*1 tablespoon Dijon-style mustard*
1 tablespoon white wine vinegar	*1 tablespoon white wine vinegar*
6 tablespoons walnut oil	*6 tablespoons walnut oil*
1 teaspoon salt	*1 teaspoon salt*
125 g/4 oz walnut halves	*1 cup walnut halves*

1. Remove the stalks from the watercress, wash, drain and place in a serving bowl.

2. Combine the mustard, vinegar, oil and salt.

3. Before serving, add the dressing and walnuts to the watercress and toss together. ·4·

Linzer Cream Tarts with Raspberry Sauce

Metric/Imperial	American
300 g/10 oz plain flour	2½ cups all-purpose flour
175 g/6 oz unsalted butter	¾ cup unsalted butter
125 g/4 oz caster sugar	½ cup sugar
2 egg yolks	2 egg yolks
Filling:	Filling:
25 g/1 oz butter	2 tablespoons butter
300 ml/½ pint single cream	1¼ cups light cream
25 g/1 oz plain flour	¼ cup all-purpose flour
50 g/2 oz caster sugar	¼ cup sugar
2 egg yolks, beaten	2 egg yolks, beaten
1 teaspoon vanilla essence	1 teaspoon vanilla
sifted icing sugar, for dredging	sifted confectioners' sugar, for dredging
Sauce:	Sauce:
500 g/1 lb raspberries	3 cups raspberries
75 g/3 oz sugar	⅓ cup sugar
1 teaspoon lemon juice	1 teaspoon lemon juice

1. To make the pastry (dough), sift the flour into a bowl and rub in (cut in) the butter until the mixture resembles fine breadcrumbs. Stir in the sugar, then the egg yolks and mix to a smooth dough. Knead lightly, then cover and chill for 30 minutes.
2. To make the custard filling, melt the butter with 175 ml/6 fl oz (¾ cup) of the cream in a small heavy saucepan. Stir together the flour, sugar and remaining cream and add to the pan. Beat well until smooth. Pour a little of the mixture on to the egg yolks and stir well, then pour into the pan. Stir over a very low heat for 5 minutes or until the custard thickens. Stir in the vanilla. Allow to cool.
3. Roll out the pastry on a floured surface and cut into 24 rounds using a 6.5 cm/2½ inch cutter. Line 12 greased tartlet tins with half the pastry rounds and prick them well with a fork.

4. Divide the filling between the 12 pastry cases (pie shells). Dampen the rims and press on the remaining pastry rounds to make lids.
5. Bake the tarts in a preheated oven (200°C/400°F), Gas Mark 6, for 10 minutes or until they are lightly browned. Transfer to a wire rack. Dredge the tops with icing (confectioners') sugar and leave to cool.
6. To make the sauce, put the raspberries, sugar and lemon juice into a blender or food processor and process for a few seconds. Sieve to remove the pips. Taste and add more sugar if necessary. ·11·

C · O · U · N · T · D · O · W · N

The day before:
Cook the chickens and carve. Cover and refrigerate. Make the ratatouille. Prepare the mayonnaise sauce and the dressing for the Watercress and Walnut Salad. Make the Linzer Cream Tarts and the Raspberry Sauce. Keep in a cool place.
On the day:
Prepare the garnishes.
To serve at 8.30 pm:
7.00: Set out the table. Place the Linzer Cream Tarts on a serving platter. Pour the Raspberry Sauce into a jug.
7.30: Chill the white wine. Cover the chicken with some of the mayonnaise and garnish. Place the remaining sauce in a bowl or gravy boat to serve separately.
8.00: Place the Chilled Ratatouille in a serving dish.
8.10: Assemble the Watercress and Walnut Salad.
8.25: Set out all the food on the table.

F · R · E · E · Z · E · R · N · O · T · E · S

Freeze the Ratatouille in rigid containers allowing headspace for expansion. Thaw at room temperature. Open freeze the Linzer Cream Tarts. Pack carefully in rigid containers. Thaw at room temperature. Make up the raspberry sauce, sieve and freeze in a rigid container allowing headspace for expansion. Thaw at room temperature.

⸗M·E·N·U⸗

· 8 ·

Oriental Supper for 2

Corn Soup
·

Barbecued Spare Ribs
Quick-fried Beans
Chinese Cabbage Salad
·

Caramel Apples

If you want to give an unusual supper for two, without putting too much strain on the budget, plan a meal with an oriental flavour.

Advance Preparation

Most of the dishes cook very quickly and should be served as soon as possible. As much of the cooking has to be done at the last moment, the planning and preparation are of particular importance. Spare (country-style) ribs are much associated with Chinese food and are great fun to eat as they are usually eaten with the fingers. In this recipe the pork is cooked in a delicious mixture of sweet and sour flavours.

Setting the Scene

The table can be given an oriental theme by using bowls to serve the food rather than large plates. China spoons for the soup and chopsticks for the rice and vegetables add to the authenticity.

China tea is often served throughout an oriental meal as it cleanses and refreshes the palate. If you wish to serve alcohol, lager or a well-chilled light white wine, like a German Mosel, would be suitable.

Corn Soup

Metric/Imperial	American
600 ml/1 pint light stock	2¹/₂ cups light stock
¹/₂ × 425 g/15 oz can cream-style sweetcorn	¹/₂ × 15 oz can cream-style corn
¹/₂ teaspoon salt	¹/₂ teaspoon salt
2 teaspoons pale dry sherry	¹/₂ tablespoon pale dry sherry
freshly ground black pepper	freshly ground black pepper
1 tablespoon cornflour, blended with 1 tablespoon water	1 tablespoon cornstarch, blended with 1 tablespoon water
1 egg, beaten	1 egg, beaten
1 spring onion, chopped, to garnish	1 scallion, chopped, for garnish

1. Place the stock in a saucepan and bring to the boil. Stir in the corn, then add the salt, sherry and pepper to taste. Add the blended cornflour (cornstarch) and simmer until thickened.
2. Lower the heat and add the beaten egg in a thin stream, stirring constantly. It is important the soup is not boiling when the egg is added.
3. Pour into warm serving bowls and garnish with the spring onion (scallion).

Barbecued Spare Ribs

Metric/Imperial	American
750 g/1¹/₂ lb pork spare ribs	1¹/₂ lb country-style pork ribs
500 ml/18 fl oz water	2¹/₄ cups water
1 tablespoon white wine vinegar or white malt vinegar	1 tablespoon white wine vinegar or white malt vinegar
Sauce:	Sauce:
1 tablespoon oil	1 tablespoon oil
1 small onion, chopped	1 small onion, chopped
1 small carrot, chopped	1 small carrot, chopped
1 tablespoon white wine	1 tablespoon white wine
vinegar or white malt vinegar	vinegar or white malt vinegar
1 tablespoon soy sauce	1 tablespoon soy sauce
1 tablespoon brown sugar	1 tablespoon brown sugar
1 tablespoon plum jam	1 tablespoon plum jam
1 teaspoon Worcestershire sauce	1 teaspoon Worcestershire sauce
1 teaspoon tomato purée	1 teaspoon tomato paste
salt	salt
freshly ground black pepper	freshly ground black pepper
spring onions, to garnish	scallions, for garnish

1. Ask the butcher for the spare (country-style) ribs to be cut into neat pieces, then remove any excess fat. Put the water and 1 tablespoon vinegar into a saucepan and bring to the boil.
2. Add the ribs and simmer for 15 minutes. Drain the meat and dry on absorbent kitchen paper.
3. Place the ribs in a good-sized roasting pan, allowing space between the pieces of meat.
4. To make the sauce, heat the oil in a saucepan and sauté the onion and carrot for 5 minutes. Add the remaining ingredients and pour over the meat.
5. Cook, uncovered, in a preheated oven (180°C/350°F), Gas Mark 4, for 20 minutes.
6. Turn the meat and baste with the sauce. Continue cooking for a further 25 minutes. Garnish with spring onions (scallions). Serve with boiled rice.

Quick-fried Beans

Metric/Imperial	American
5 tablespoons chicken stock	¹/₃ cup chicken stock
250 g/8 oz French beans	¹/₂ lb green beans
1¹/₂ tablespoons vegetable oil	1¹/₂ tablespoons vegetable oil
15 g/¹/₂ oz butter	1 tablespoon butter
2-3 cloves garlic, peeled and crushed	2-3 cloves garlic, peeled and crushed
1 spring onion, sliced	1 scallion, sliced
¹/₂ teaspoon salt	¹/₂ teaspoon salt

2 teaspoons soy sauce
1/2 teaspoon sugar
2 teaspoons pale dry sherry

2 teaspoons soy sauce
1/2 teaspoon sugar
2 teaspoons pale dry sherry

1. Place the stock in a large saucepan and bring to the boil. Add the beans and simmer until all the liquid has evaporated, turning them constantly.
2. Heat the oil and butter in a wok or frying pan (skillet) and stir-fry the garlic and spring onion (scallion) with the salt for 30 seconds.
3. Add the beans and stir-fry for 15 seconds.
4. Sprinkle with the soy sauce, sugar and sherry, then stir-fry for a further minute. Transfer to a warm serving dish.

Barbecued spare ribs

Chinese Cabbage Salad

Metric/Imperial
250 g/8 oz Chinese cabbage
  or hard white cabbage,
  shredded
Dressing:
2 tablespoons soy sauce
pinch of salt
1 tablespoon sugar
1 tablespoon sesame oil

American
1/2 lb bok choy or hard
  white cabbage, shredded
Dressing:
2 tablespoons soy sauce
pinch of salt
1 tablespoon sugar
1 tablespoon sesame oil

1. Blanch the cabbage in boiling water for 2 to 3 minutes. Drain and place in a serving bowl.
2. Mix together the dressing ingredients. Pour over the cabbage and toss well. Serve warm. ·4·10·

Caramel Apples

Metric/Imperial	American
2 eating apples, peeled, cored and quartered	*2 dessert apples, peeled, cored and quartered*
15 g/½ oz plain flour	*2 tablespoons all-purpose flour*
1½ teaspoons cornflour	*1½ teaspoons cornstarch*
1 egg white	*1 egg white*
oil for deep-frying	*oil for deep-frying*
75 g/3 oz sugar	*⅓ cup sugar*
1½ tablespoons water	*1½ tablespoons water*
2 teaspoons sesame seeds	*2 teaspoons sesame seeds*

1. Dust the apple quarters lightly with a little of the flour. Sift the remaining flour and cornflour (cornstarch) into a bowl. Add the egg white and mix to a smooth paste.

2. Heat the oil in a wok or deep-fryer to 180°C/350°F. Coat the apple quarters, one at a time, with the paste, then drop them carefully into the oil. Fry until golden brown. Drain on absorbent kitchen paper.

3. Place the sugar and water in a small saucepan and stir until dissolved. Bring to the boil and boil until the syrup is a light golden brown.

4. Stir in the apple quarters and sesame seeds. Transfer to lightly oiled individual serving dishes.

5. A bowl of cold water may be placed on the table, so the apple pieces can be picked up with chopsticks and lowered into the water before eating, to harden the caramel. ·10·

C·O·U·N·T·D·O·W·N

The day before:
Prepare the Corn Soup to the end of stage 1 and store in a covered container in the refrigerator.

On the day:
Make the sauce for the Barbecued Spare Ribs. Cool, cover and refrigerate until required. Trim the spare ribs of excess fat and simmer. Drain, discard the liquid, and place in a roasting pan. Cover and refrigerate. Prepare the French (green) beans, place in a polythene (plastic) bag and refrigerate. Wash and shred the Chinese cabbage (bok choy) and store in a covered container. Make the cornflour (cornstarch) paste for the Caramel Apples and refrigerate. Place the sugar and water in a small pan for the caramel.

To serve at 8 pm:
6.30: Prepare the table.
6.50: Preheat the oven.
7.00: Chill the lager or wine.
7.10: Pour the sauce over the spare (country-style) ribs and place in the oven.
7.15: Remove the cornflour paste from the refrigerator. Assemble all the ingredients for the Caramel Apples.
7.30: Turn the spare ribs. Prepare the spring onion (scallion) for the beans.
7.35: Bring the stock to the boil and add the beans. Blanch the cabbage, drain and toss in the dressing. Keep warm.
7.45: Stir-fry the garlic and spring onion in the wok. Add the beans, stir-fry and keep warm.
7.50: Reheat the soup and add the beaten egg stirring all the time.
7.55: Garnish the spare ribs.
8.00: Serve the Corn Soup.
About 8.45: Make the dessert after the main course. Serve immediately.

F·R·E·E·Z·E·R · N·O·T·E·S

The spare ribs can be frozen for up to 2 months. Wrap individually or interleave with wax paper, then overwrap and seal. Thaw in the refrigerator then reheat, covered, in a preheated oven (180°C/350°F), Gas Mark 4, for 20 to 25 minutes.

Cook's Tip:
Soy sauce is used as a flavouring in Chinese dishes and extra can be placed in a small bowl on the table for added seasoning. This can be used by each diner as an additional dip.

M · E · N · U

· 9 ·

French Cuisine for 6

Potage Crécy

·

Lamb Noisettes
Potatoes Lyonnaise
Tian de Courgettes

·

Tarte Bordaloue

For a really enjoyable dinner party it is a good idea to have a theme. French food is always popular and should appeal to most palates. Contrary to belief, most dishes are not difficult to prepare.

Serving the French Way
In order fully to appreciate the food, the French serve the meat and any sauces alone, with the vegetables following as a separate course. Therefore, good-quality meat is very important to them. Often a green salad is served at the end of the main course. This can be as simple as lettuce or endive (chicory), but can also include some watercress and cucumber all tossed in a French dressing.

Cheeses to Choose
To extend the meal, it is very French to serve a cheese course before the dessert. A small selection of cheeses such as a Brie, a blue, a chèvre (goat) and a fresh cheese provides a reasonable choice.

A dry white wine would go well with the Lamb Noisettes. If you are feeling extravagant, a sweet champagne would be an excellent dessert wine.

Potage Crécy

Metric/Imperial	American
50 g/2 oz butter	1/4 cup butter
2 onions, thinly sliced	2 onions, thinly sliced
2 litres/3 1/2 pints chicken stock	4 1/2 pints/9 cups chicken stock
1 kg/2 lb small young carrots, sliced into thin rounds	2 lb small young carrots, sliced into thin rounds
salt	salt
freshly ground black pepper	freshly ground black pepper
3 tablespoons long-grain rice	3 tablespoons long-grain rice
120 ml/4 fl oz double cream	1/2 cup heavy cream

1. Melt half the butter in a heavy saucepan and gently sauté the onions for 5 minutes until soft. Add the stock and carrots and bring to the boil. Lower the heat, season, then simmer for 1 1/2 hours.
2. Stir in the rice and simmer for a further 30 minutes or until the rice is tender.
3. Work the soup through the medium blade of a *mouli-légumes* (vegetable mill) or purée in a blender or food processor.
4. Return the soup to the rinsed-out pan, add the cream and the remaining butter and reheat gently, stirring constantly. Taste and adjust the seasoning.
5. Pour the hot soup into a warm soup tureen and serve immediately. ·2·10·

Lamb Noisettes

Metric/Imperial	American
75 g/3 oz butter	1/3 cup butter
1 1/2 tablespoons oil	1 1/2 tablespoons oil
12 noisettes of lamb, prepared from the loin	12 boneless double loin lamb chops
1 large onion, finely chopped	1 large onion, finely chopped
1-2 cloves garlic, peeled and crushed	1-2 cloves garlic, peeled and crushed
750 g/1 1/2 lb tomatoes, skinned and chopped	1 1/2 lb tomatoes, skinned and chopped
1 1/2 tablespoons tomato purée	1 1/2 tablespoons tomato paste
200 ml/1/3 pint dry white wine	7/8 cup dry white wine
salt	salt
freshly ground black pepper	freshly ground black pepper
fresh mint sprigs, to garnish	fresh mint sprigs, to garnish

1. Heat half the butter and half the oil in a pan and sauté the lamb for about 15 minutes.
2. Meanwhile, heat the remaining butter and oil in another pan and gently sauté the onion and garlic until soft. Add the tomatoes, tomato purée (paste) and wine to the onion and bring to the boil, stirring.
3. Cook, uncovered, over high heat for 10 to 15 minutes, stirring occasionally. Add salt and pepper to taste.
4. Place the lamb on a warm serving dish and pour over the sauce. Garnish with fresh mint. ·10·

Potatoes Lyonnaise

Metric/Imperial	American
1 kg/2 lb potatoes	2 lb potatoes
50 g/2 oz butter	1/4 cup butter
2 onions, thinly sliced	2 onions, thinly sliced
salt	salt
freshly ground black pepper	freshly ground black pepper
To Garnish:	For Garnish:
chopped parsley	chopped parsley
chopped chives	chopped chives

1. Blanch the potatoes in a saucepan of boiling water for 1 minute, then drain.
2. Melt the butter in a pan and sauté the onions for 5 minutes.

3. Thinly slice the potatoes and layer them with the onions, salt and pepper, in a greased 1 litre/2 pint (1 quart) casserole dish, finishing with potatoes. Cover the casserole.

4. Cook in a preheated oven (200°C/400°F), Gas Mark 6, for 1 hour. Remove the lid and continue to cook for 30 minutes to allow the potatoes to brown.

5. Mix together the parsley and chives, then sprinkle over the potatoes before serving.

Tian de Courgettes

Metric/Imperial	American
4 tablespoons olive oil	1/4 cup olive oil
1 kg/2 lb courgettes, thinly sliced	2 lb zucchini, thinly sliced
2 cloves garlic, peeled	2 garlic cloves, peeled
salt	salt
freshly ground black pepper	freshly ground black pepper
1 egg, beaten	1 egg, beaten
50 g/2 oz fresh breadcrumbs	1 cup fresh bread crumbs
50 g/2 oz Gruyère cheese, grated	1/2 cup grated Gruyère cheese

1. Heat half the oil in a large heavy pan and sauté the courgettes (zucchini) and garlic with a little salt and pepper over a moderate heat for 5 minutes.

2. Discard the garlic, then leave the courgettes to cool slightly. Stir in the beaten egg and reheat gently. Taste and adjust the seasoning.

3. Transfer the vegetables to an oiled gratin dish and level the surface. Mix together the breadcrumbs and cheese, sprinkle over the top, then sprinkle with the remaining oil.

4. Cook, uncovered, in a preheated oven (200°C/400°F), Gas Mark 6, for 15 minutes or until golden brown. ·3·

Tarte bordaloue with greengage and brandy sauce

Tarte Bordaloue

Metric/Imperial	American
325 g/11 oz plain flour	2¾ cups all-purpose flour
200 g/7 oz butter	¾ cup plus 2 tablespoons butter
125 g/4 oz icing sugar, sifted	1 scant cup sifted confectioners' sugar
1 egg	1 egg
Filling:	Filling:
350 g/12 oz full-fat soft cheese	1½ cups full-fat curd cheese
2 eggs	2 eggs
15 g/½ oz cornflour	2 tablespoons cornstarch
grated rind of ½ lemon	grated rind of ½ lemon
1 tablespoon lemon juice	1 tablespoon lemon juice
50 g/2 oz caster sugar	¼ cup sugar
25 g/1 oz ground almonds	¼ cup ground almonds
1.25 kg/2½ lb greengages, quartered and stoned	2½ lb greengages, quartered and pitted
40 g/1½ oz demerara sugar	¼ cup brown or raw sugar
Sauce:	Sauce:
750 g/1½ lb greengages, stoned and chopped	1½ lb greengages, pitted and chopped
4 tablespoons water	4 tablespoons water
75 g/3 oz sugar	⅓ cup sugar
4 tablespoons brandy	4 tablespoons brandy

1. To make the pastry (dough), sift the flour into a bowl. Rub in (cut in) the butter until the mixture resembles fine breadcrumbs. Stir in the sugar. Add the egg and mix to a dough. Knead the pastry lightly in the bowl. Cover with cling film (plastic wrap) or foil and chill for at least 1 hour.
2. Meanwhile, make the filling. Beat the cheese until softened and beat in the eggs, one at a time. Beat in the cornflour (cornstarch) then the lemon rind and juice, sugar and ground almonds.
3. Roll out the pastry on a lightly floured board and use to line a greased 25 cm/10 inch flan tin. Trim the edges and prick the bottom all over with a fork. Spread the filling in the pastry case (pie shell).
4. Arrange the greengage segments in overlapping rings, skin side down, on the filling. (The effect resembles a water lily.) Sprinkle with brown sugar.
5. Bake in a preheated oven (200°C/400°F), Gas Mark 6, for 30 to 35 minutes. Cover the top with foil towards the end of the cooking time if it is browning too much. Allow to cool on a wire rack.
6. To make the sauce, place the greengages and water in a saucepan and cook for about 15 minutes or until soft. Rub through a sieve and return the purée to the pan. Add the sugar and stir over a low heat until dissolved. Bring to the boil and simmer for 5 minutes. Stir in the brandy and leave to cool. Serve the sauce with the cold tart. ·3·

C · O · U · N · T · D · O · W · N

The day before:
Make the Potage Crécy to the end of stage 3. Make the tomato sauce. Prepare the breadcrumbs for the Tian de Courgettes and grate the cheese. Prepare the pastry and the sauce for the Tarte Bordaloue.

On the day:
Prepare the French bread and wrap in foil. Assemble the Potatoes Lyonnaise, cover and refrigerate. Prepare the courgettes (zucchini) and make up to the end of stage 3. Bake the Tarte Bordaloue. Cool and refrigerate until required. Prepare the table.

To serve at 8 pm:
6.10: Preheat the oven.
6.30: Cook the Potatoes Lyonnaise.
7.30: Cook the Lamb Noisettes and place on a serving dish. Heat the sauce and pour over. Cover and keep warm. Uncover the potatoes.
7.45: Place the courgettes (zucchini) in the oven with the French bread.
7.55: Garnish the lamb. Finish the soup.

F · R · E · E · Z · E · R · N · O · T · E · S

None of the dishes is suitable for freezing.

MENU

· 10 ·

Midsummer Dinner for 2

Artichoke and Hazelnut Soup
·
Chicken Kiev
Baby Onions in Tomato Sauce
Marinated Courgettes
·
Red Berry Salad

With an elegant meal for two, there is every excuse to create a really romantic setting. Use a white or pastel tablecloth and napkins, perhaps with a touch of lace; delicate china and glassware; elegant candlestick holders with flower rings at the base of the candle and a small summer flower arrangement.

If it is a really warm evening, serve the soup chilled with an ice cube in the bowl. The toasted hazelnuts add a delicious nutty texture and flavour. If liked serve the soup with brown bread and butter or rolls.

The Onions in Tomato Sauce make a pleasant contrast to the hot chicken as they are served chilled. Courgettes (zucchini) are given a different treatment, served raw and marinated with spring onions (scallions) and capers.

Soft Summer Fruits

A light fruit dessert is all that is required after this meal. Redcurrants, raspberries and strawberries served together in a sugar syrup make an ideal summer dessert. A sparkling wine would fit this meal and occasion — either Asti Spumante or Champagne, well chilled.

Artichoke and Hazelnut Soup

Metric/Imperial	American
75 g/3 oz hazelnuts, lightly toasted	2/3 cup lightly toasted hazelnuts
1 × 400 g/14 oz can globe artichoke hearts	1 × 16 oz can globe artichoke hearts
1 small onion, chopped	1 small onion, chopped
450 ml/3/4 pint chicken stock	2 cups chicken stock
15 g/1/2 oz butter	1 tablespoon butter
1 tablespoon plain flour	1 tablespoon all-purpose flour
150 ml/1/4 pint single cream	2/3 cup light cream
salt	salt
freshly ground black pepper	freshly ground black pepper
To Garnish:	For Garnish:
1 tablespoon lightly toasted and chopped hazelnuts	1 tablespoon lightly toasted and chopped hazelnuts
watercress sprigs	watercress sprigs

1. Put the hazelnuts into a blender or food processor and crush them coarsely. Transfer to a saucepan.
2. Drain the liquid from the artichoke hearts and add to the pan. Roughly chop three of the artichoke hearts and add to the pan with the onion and chicken stock. Bring to the boil and simmer for 20 minutes.
3. Allow to cool, then strain the stock.
4. Melt the butter in a saucepan and stir in the flour. Cook for 1 minute, stirring. Gradually stir in the stock. Finely chop the remaining artichoke hearts and add. Simmer gently for 20 minutes. Cool slightly.
5. Purée the soup in the blender or food processor until smooth. Pour the soup into a clean saucepan. Stir in the cream and heat through gently. Add salt and pepper to taste. Serve in soup cups or bowls, garnished with the chopped hazelnuts and watercress. If liked, the soup can be served chilled. ·2·8·

Chicken Kiev

Metric/Imperial	American
2 suprêmes of chicken (breast with part of wing bone)	2 suprêmes of chicken (breast with part of wing bone)
salt	salt
freshly ground black pepper	freshly ground black pepper
oil for deep-frying	oil for deep-frying
watercress, to garnish	watercress, to garnish
Kiev Butter:	Kiev Butter:
50 g/2 oz butter	1/4 cup butter
1 tablespoon chopped fresh parsley	1 tablespoon chopped fresh parsley
lemon juice	lemon juice
Coating:	Coating:
1 tablespoon plain flour	1 tablespoon all-purpose flour
salt	salt
freshly ground black pepper	freshly ground black pepper
1 egg, beaten	1 egg, beaten
3 tablespoons fresh breadcrumbs	3 tablespoons soft bread crumbs

1. Place the chicken between two pieces of cling film (plastic wrap) and beat as flat as possible. Season.
2. To make the Kiev butter, blend all the ingredients together until smooth. Shape into a roll 7.5 cm/3 inches long, wrap in cling film and chill.
3. With a sharp-pointed knife, cut a pocket in the fleshy part of the chicken pieces. Insert half the butter in each, tapering the ends to fit neatly. Tuck the flesh over and secure with wooden cocktail sticks.
4. Season the flour with salt and pepper and use to dust the chicken suprêmes. Dip in the beaten egg and then in the breadcrumbs to coat evenly.
5. Heat the oil in a deep-fryer to 180°C/350°F and fry the chicken for 15 minutes or until cooked.
6. Drain on absorbent kitchen paper and place on a warm serving dish. Garnish with watercress. ·9·

Baby Onions in Tomato Sauce

Metric/Imperial	American
1 tablespoon oil	1 tablespoon oil
½ small onion, finely chopped	½ small onion, finely chopped
150 ml/¼ pint red wine	⅔ cup red wine
1 tablespoon vinegar	1 tablespoon vinegar
1 tablespoon tomato purée	1 tablespoon tomato paste
1 teaspoon brown sugar	1 teaspoon brown sugar
salt	salt
freshly ground black pepper	freshly ground black pepper
2 teaspoons chopped fresh herbs	2 teaspoons chopped fresh herbs
125 g/4 oz small button onions, peeled	¼ lb small button onions, peeled

1. Heat the oil in a saucepan and gently sauté the chopped onion for 3 minutes. Add the red wine, vinegar, tomato purée (paste), sugar, salt and pepper to taste, and the herbs. Bring to the boil and simmer gently for 5 minutes. The mixture should be well reduced and a rich-red colour.
2. Add the button onions. Cover and cook gently until the onions are just tender. Test with a skewer after 10 to 15 minutes. It should pierce the onions quite easily.
3. Cool, cover and chill. ·1·

Chicken Kiev with parsley butter

Marinated Courgettes

Metric/Imperial	American
250 g/8 oz courgettes, thinly sliced	1/2 lb zucchini, thinly sliced
3 spring onions, finely chopped	3 scallions, finely chopped
1 tablespoon chopped chives	1 tablespoon chopped chives
4 tablespoons olive oil	4 tablespoons olive oil
1/2-1 tablespoon white wine vinegar	1/2-1 tablespoon white wine vinegar
salt	salt
freshly ground black pepper	freshly ground black pepper
1/2-1 tablespoon capers	1/2-1 tablespoon capers

1. Mix the courgettes (zucchini) with the spring onions (scallions) and chopped chives in a salad bowl.
2. Mix the olive oil with the wine vinegar, salt and pepper to taste, then add the capers.
3. Stir the dressing into the salad ingredients, so that the courgettes are evenly coated. Allow the salad to stand in a cool place for at least 1 hour for the flavours to mingle. ·4·

Red Berry Salad

Metric/Imperial	American
250 ml/8 fl oz water	1 cup water
75 g/3 oz caster sugar	1/3 cup sugar
125 g/4 oz fresh redcurrants, stalks removed	1 cup fresh red currants, stalks removed
250 g/8 oz strawberries, hulled	1 1/2 cups strawberries, hulled
125 g/4 oz raspberries	3/4 cup raspberries
natural yogurt, to serve	unflavored yogurt, to serve

1. Heat the water and sugar in a saucepan until the sugar dissolves, then boil for 3 minutes.
2. Remove from the heat and cool for 5 minutes. Stir in the redcurrants and leave until cold.
3. Add the strawberries and raspberries. Mix well and spoon into a serving bowl. Serve chilled with natural (unflavored) yogurt.

C · O · U · N · T · D · O · W · N

The day before:
Make the Artichoke and Hazelnut Soup without the cream. Toast the hazelnuts for the garnish and store in an airtight container. Make the Kiev Butter and refrigerate. Prepare the Baby Onions in Tomato Sauce, place in the serving dish, cover and chill in the refrigerator. Make the sugar syrup and add the redcurrants. Keep refrigerated overnight.

On the day:
Prepare the Chicken Kiev, place on a plate in the refrigerator. Make up the Marinated Courgettes. Cover and keep cool. Prepare the raspberries and strawberries, add to the redcurrants and stir. Chill until required.

To serve at 8.00 pm:
6.30: Prepare the table.
7.00: Chill the wine. Place the soup in a pan if serving hot. Prepare the watercress.
7.15: Place the cream or yogurt for the dessert in a jug or bowl.
7.40: Heat the oil for the Chicken Kiev.
7.45: Cook the Chicken Kiev. Drain and keep warm.
7.55: Reheat the soup, adding the cream, then garnish and serve. Garnish the chicken before serving.

F · R · E · E · Z · E · R · N · O · T · E · S

The Chicken Kiev will freeze if the suprêmes have not been previously frozen. This is very important. Do make sure you use fresh chicken if you are intending to freeze it. Freeze uncooked. Thaw overnight in the refrigerator. Cook as directed. The Red Berry Salad is suitable for freezing. The fruit will be softer but quite acceptable. Place in a rigid container allowing headspace. Thaw in the refrigerator overnight.

MENU

· 11 ·

Formal Entertaining for 8

Rack of Lamb in Pastry
Red Cabbage with Chestnuts

·

Franklin's Potatoes

·

Pear Galette

This elegant menu is suitable for more formal occasions such as a special celebration or business entertaining. As most of the dishes are hot and it is a fairly rich meal, it would be more appropriate for serving during the winter months. Serve Baby Onions in Tomato Sauce (see previous menu) if a starter is required.

Simple and Sophisticated

A formal dinner party requires an elegant table setting. Here is a chance to use a pretty, delicate tablecloth and your best china, silverware and glassware. If space permits, cutlery should be placed in order of use, on each side of the tablemat. Tall elegant candlesticks, cloth napkins and a small simple flower arrangement can add to the effect. Choose a particular colour scheme for the table; pale plain colours give a more sophisticated effect than too much pattern.

Place coffee cups and liqueur glasses ready on a side table, with any available liqueurs, chocolates or petits fours. The rack of lamb deserves a good red wine such as Châteauneuf-du-Pape. A sweet Vouvray would be a suitable white wine for the dessert. A dessert wine such as this should always be well-chilled before serving.

Rack of Lamb in Pastry

Metric/Imperial

2 joints of best end of lamb
50 g/2 oz butter
1 tablespoon oil
500 g/1 lb frozen puff
  pastry, thawed
beaten egg, to glaze
Filling:
25 g/1 oz butter
1 medium onion, finely
  chopped
2 cloves garlic, peeled and
  crushed
6 lambs' kidneys, skinned,
  cored and finely chopped
175 g/6 oz mushrooms,
  finely chopped
25 g/1 oz pine nuts
2 tablespoons chopped fresh
  parsley
2 tablespoons red wine
salt
freshly ground black pepper
To Garnish:
1 orange, cut into wedges
watercress sprigs

American

2 joints of rib lamb chops
1/4 cup butter
1 tablespoon oil
1 lb frozen puff dough,
  thawed
beaten egg, to glaze
Filling:
2 tablespoons butter
1 medium onion, finely
  chopped
2 cloves garlic, peeled and
  crushed
6 lamb kidneys, skinned,
  cored and finely chopped
1 1/2 cups finely chopped
  mushrooms
1/4 cup pine nuts
2 tablespoons chopped fresh
  parsley
2 tablespoons red wine
salt
freshly ground black pepper
For Garnish:
1 orange, cut into wedges
watercress sprigs

1. Trim the excess fat and meat from the tip of the bones, leaving about 7.5 cm/3 inches of bone exposed. Using a darning needle and fine twine, sew the 2 joints of lamb together to make a long rack.
2. Melt the butter with the oil in a roasting tin. Put the lamb in the tin and roast in a preheated oven (190°C/375°F), Gas Mark 5, for 10 minutes. Remove the lamb from the tin and allow to cool.
3. To make the filling, melt the butter in a frying pan (skillet) and sauté the onion and garlic over a moderate heat for 3 to 4 minutes, stirring occasionally. Add the kidneys and stir-fry for 2 to 3 minutes.

Red Cabbage with chestnuts; Franklin's potatoes, a delicious vegetable combination.

Add the mushrooms and pine nuts. Stir well and cook for 5 minutes. Stir in the parsley and wine, add salt and pepper to taste and bring to the boil. Boil for 2 to 3 minutes. Allow to cool.

4. Spread the kidney filling over both sides of the meat and press it on well to form a thick coating.

5. Roll out the pastry on a floured board to a rectangle, about 36 × 30 cm/14 × 12 inches. Place the rack of lamb on its side on the pastry and push the bones through the pastry. Press the pastry close to the meat. Bring round the edges and join them to form a neat seal at the ends and under the chops. Trim the ends. Re-roll the trimmings and cut out leaf shapes. Brush with beaten egg, arrange the leaves in a pattern and brush again with egg.

6. Stand the lamb on a baking sheet. Increase the oven temperature to (230°C/450°F), Gas Mark 8, and cook for 10 minutes, then reduce the temperature to (190°C/375°F), Gas Mark 5, and cook for a further 15 to 20 minutes or until browned. Serve hot, garnished with orange and watercress.

Red Cabbage with Chestnuts

Metric/Imperial	American
500 g/1 lb chestnuts	1 lb chestnuts
175 g/6 oz prunes, soaked overnight, stoned and roughly chopped	1 cup prunes, soaked overnight, pitted and roughly chopped
175 g/6 oz cooking apples, peeled and chopped	1½ cups peeled, cored and chopped tart apples
1 medium onion, chopped	1 medium onion, chopped
1 kg/2 lb red cabbage, shredded	2 lb red cabbage, shredded
salt	salt
freshly ground black pepper	freshly ground black pepper
1 tablespoon sugar	1 tablespoon sugar
2 tablespoons cider vinegar	2 tablespoons cider vinegar
200 ml/7 fl oz beef stock	⅞ cup beef stock

1. Prick the chestnuts and cook in a saucepan of boiling water for 20 minutes. Drain and leave until cool enough to handle, then peel and halve.

2. In a casserole, make layers of the chestnuts, prunes, apple, onion and red cabbage. Season.

3. Combine the sugar, vinegar and stock and pour over the vegetables.

4. Cook in a preheated oven (150°C/300°F), Gas Mark 2, for 2 hours, stirring occasionally. If too bland, add a little more vinegar and sugar.

Franklin's Potatoes

Metric/Imperial	American
450 ml/¾ pint milk	1⅞ cups milk
½ onion, studded with 4 cloves	½ onion, studded with 4 cloves
blade of mace	blade of mace
1 bay leaf	1 bay leaf
parsley stalk	parsley stalk
6 whole black peppercorns	6 whole black peppercorns
125 g/4 oz fresh breadcrumbs	2 cups soft bread crumbs
25 g/1 oz butter	2 tablespoons butter
2 tablespoons double cream	2 tablespoons heavy cream
salt	salt
freshly ground black pepper	freshly ground black pepper
750 g/1½ lb new or firm potatoes, thinly sliced	1½ lb new or firm potatoes, thinly sliced
sprig fresh bay, to garnish	sprig fresh bay, for garnish

1. Put the milk into a saucepan with the onion, mace, bay leaf, parsley stalk and peppercorns. Warm over a gentle heat, then remove from the heat and leave to infuse for 20 minutes. Strain.

2. In a bowl, combine the breadcrumbs, butter and cream with the milk. Beat well with a wooden spoon until the sauce is smooth, then season.

3. Grease a small casserole. Arrange layers of potatoes in the casserole, pouring a little sauce between each layer, finishing with sauce.

4. Bake in a preheated oven (190°C/375°F), Gas Mark 5, for about 1¼ hours or until the potatoes are tender when pierced with a sharp knife. (While the oven temperature is raised to brown the Rack of Lamb in Pastry, remove the potatoes and return when the temperature is reduced.)

5. Before serving, garnish with a sprig of bay. ·2·

Pear Galette

Metric/Imperial	American
50 g/2 oz hazelnuts	½ cup hazelnuts
350 g/12 oz plain flour	3 cups all-purpose flour
125 g/4 oz caster sugar	½ cup sugar
250 g/8 oz butter	1 cup butter
300 ml/½ pint double cream	1¼ cups heavy cream
8 canned pear halves, drained	8 canned pear halves, drained
a few whole hazelnuts	a few whole hazelnuts

1. Skin and finely chop the hazelnuts.

2. Sift the flour into a bowl and add the sugar and nuts; rub in (cut in) the butter very lightly. There is a high proportion of butter to the amount of flour, but the sugar and nuts help to prevent the mixture from becoming too sticky.

3. Divide the mixture in half, press into two lined 20 cm/8 inch sandwich tins (layer cake pans) and prick with a fork. Bake in the centre of a preheated oven (190°C/375°F), Gas Mark 5, for 20 minutes or until the nut mixture is just beginning to change colour, then lower the oven temperature to 160°C/325°F, Gas Mark 3, and bake for 15 to 20 minutes.

4. Allow the hazelnut rounds to cool for 5 minutes. Turn out very carefully on to a wire rack. Mark one round into 8 portions while still warm. When cool, store in an airtight container.

5. To serve, whip the cream until thick. Place the unmarked hazelnut round on a serving plate, top with half the cream and the pears (place these with the cut side downwards) and press a whole hazelnut into each pear.

6. Place the second hazelnut round over the pears. Pipe the remaining cream on top of the galette and decorate with whole hazelnuts. ·7·

C·O·U·N·T·D·O·W·N

Two days before:
Soak the prunes.

The day before:
Make the filling for the lamb and refrigerate. Make up the Red Cabbage with Chestnuts. Cool and refrigerate. Skin the hazelnuts and chop. Make the hazelnut rounds for the Pear Galette. Cool, pack and store in an airtight container.

On the day:
Brown the rack of lamb in the oven, cool and coat with the filling. Roll out the pastry (dough) and cover the rack. Refrigerate. Infuse the milk for Franklin's Potatoes and make up the sauce. Place in a bowl, cover and refrigerate. Set the table, arrange the flowers, etc.

To serve at 8 pm:
6.00: Open the red wine. Assemble and decorate the Pear Galette then place in the refrigerator. Prepare the orange and watercress garnish. Cover and store in the refrigerator until required.

6.15: Preheat the oven. Slice the potatoes and assemble the Franklin's Potatoes.

6.30: Place the potatoes in the oven.

7.15: Reheat the Red Cabbage with Chestnuts.

7.25: Remove the potatoes from the oven and raise the temperature.

7.30: Brush the lamb rack with egg glaze and place in the oven.

7.40: Reduce oven temperature. Return the potatoes to the oven.

8.00: Serve starter if included.

F·R·E·E·Z·E·R· N·O·T·E·S

None of the dishes is suitable for freezing.

M·E·N·U

· 12 ·

Garden Party for 12

Spinach Pancakes with Ham and Mushrooms
Herb Pancakes with Chicken Filling

·

Raspberry and Hazelnut Roll

During the summer it is a good idea to make use of the garden when entertaining large parties.

Seating Arrangements

Guests can be seated, but it is more usual and more fun to serve the food buffet-style. Set the table inside if you are doubtful about the weather. People can then circulate outside and sit in the sun or shade.

Choosing the Right Food

To enable as much time as possible to be spent with guests, it is important to choose a menu in which most of the food is prepared in advance.

Pancakes (crêpes) are ideal as they can be made beforehand and stored in the refrigerator or frozen, filled or unfilled, then reheated before serving.

Light salads are the most suitable accompaniments for warm-weather meals. A crisp, mixed green salad could be served with a fresh herb vinaigrette or a simple salad of sliced tomatoes, onions and chives.

Suitable Summer Drinks

A sangria or fruit punch, or a white wine such as an Italian dry Soave or a German Piesporter, would be suitable for this meal.

E·N·T·E·R·T·A·I·N·I·N·G

Spinach Pancakes with Ham and Mushrooms

Metric/Imperial
75 g/3 oz plain flour
1 teaspoon salt
2 eggs
200 ml/7 fl oz milk
75 g/3 oz butter, melted
250 g/8 oz frozen spinach,
    thawed and liquidized
pinch of grated nutmeg
oil for frying
25 g/1 oz Parmesan cheese,
    grated
Filling:
40 g/1½ oz butter
1 small onion, finely
    chopped
125 g/4 oz mushrooms,
    chopped
1 tablespoon plain flour
300 ml/½ pint single
    cream
125 g/4 oz cooked lean
    ham, finely chopped
1 tablespoon chopped fresh
    parsley
freshly ground black pepper

American
¾ cup all-purpose flour
1 teaspoon salt
2 eggs
⅞ cup milk
⅓ cup melted butter
1 cup spinach purée
pinch of grated nutmeg
oil for frying
¼ cup grated Parmesan
    cheese
Filling:
3 tablespoons butter
1 small onion, finely
    chopped
1 cup chopped mushrooms
1 tablespoon all-purpose
    flour
1¼ cups light cream
½ cup finely chopped lean
    cooked cured ham
1 tablespoon chopped fresh
    parsley
freshly ground black pepper

1. Sift the flour and salt into a bowl. Beat in the eggs. Gradually beat in the milk and then 25 g/1 oz (2 tablespoons) of the melted butter. Stir in the spinach purée and nutmeg. Cover the bowl and leave the batter to stand for at least 1 hour.
2. To make the filling, melt the butter in a small saucepan and sauté the onion and mushrooms over a moderate heat for 3 minutes, stirring occasionally. Stir in the flour and cook for 1 minute, then gradually pour on the cream, stirring constantly.

Bring to the boil, stirring, and simmer for 2 minutes. Stir in the ham, parsley and pepper to taste.
3. Make the pancakes as described in stages 3 and 4 of the Herb Pancakes with Chicken Filling. (See following recipe.)
4. Divide the filling between the pancakes, spreading it in a line along the centre. Roll up the pancakes. Arrange them in a greased baking dish and brush with the remaining melted butter. Sprinkle the pancakes with the cheese.
5. Reheat the pancakes in a preheated oven (180°C/350°F), Gas Mark 4, for 15 to 20 minutes.

Herb Pancakes with Chicken Filling

Metric/Imperial	American
125 g/4 oz plain flour	1 cup all-purpose flour
1 teaspoon salt	1 teaspoon salt
1 egg	1 egg
1 egg yolk	1 egg yolk
275 ml/9 fl oz milk	1 generous cup milk
75 g/3 oz butter, melted	1/3 cup melted butter
2 tablespoons chopped fresh parsley	2 tablespoons chopped fresh parsley
1 teaspoon dried tarragon	1 teaspoon dried tarragon
oil for frying	oil for frying
Filling:	Filling:
250 g/8 oz cottage cheese	1 cup cottage cheese
250 g/8 oz full-fat soft cheese	1 cup full-fat curd cheese
2 eggs, beaten	2 eggs, beaten
250 g/8 oz cooked chicken meat, finely chopped	1 cup finely chopped cooked chicken meat
1 tablespoon chopped fresh parsley	1 tablespoon chopped fresh parsley
salt	salt
freshly ground black pepper	freshly ground black pepper
pinch of cayenne	pinch of cayenne
25 g/1 oz Parmesan cheese, grated	1/4 cup grated Parmesan cheese

1. Sift the flour and salt into a bowl. Beat in the egg and egg yolk. Gradually beat in the milk and then 25 g/1 oz (2 tablespoons) of the melted butter. Cover the bowl and leave the batter to stand for 1 hour.
2. To make the filling, beat together the cottage cheese, soft (curd) cheese and eggs. Stir in the chicken and parsley, then season. Set aside.
3. Stir the parsley and tarragon into the batter. Heat

Spinach pancakes with ham and mushrooms; Herb pancakes with chicken filling

a 12.5 cm/5 inch frying pan (skillet) and lightly brush the bottom with oil. Pour in about 2 tablespoons of the batter and tilt the pan so that the batter covers the bottom evenly. Cook over a moderate heat until bubbles appear on the surface of the pancake. Flip or turn it over and cook the other side until golden brown. If possible, use two pans to halve the cooking time.
4. As each pancake is cooked, place it on a plate lined with greaseproof (waxed) paper.
5. Divide the filling between the pancakes, spreading it in a line along the centre. Roll up the pancakes. Arrange them in a greased baking dish and brush with the remaining melted butter. Sprinkle the pancakes with the cheese.
6. Reheat the pancakes in a preheated oven (180°C/350°F), Gas Mark 4, for 15 minutes. ·7·

Raspberry and Hazelnut Roll

Metric/Imperial	American
6 eggs	6 eggs
250 g/8 oz caster sugar	1 cup sugar
125 g/4 oz plain flour, sifted	1 cup sifted all-purpose flour
125 g/4 oz ground hazelnuts, toasted	1 cup toasted ground hazelnuts
2 tablespoons vegetable oil	2 tablespoons vegetable oil
caster sugar, for dredging	sugar, for dredging
Filling:	Filling:
450 ml/3/4 pint double cream	2 cups heavy cream
500 g/1 lb raspberries	1 lb raspberries
2 tablespoons icing sugar, sifted	2 tablespoons confectioners' sugar, sifted
To Serve:	To Serve:
175 ml/6 fl oz double cream, whipped	3/4 cup heavy cream, whipped
16 raspberries (optional)	16 raspberries (optional)

1. Grease two 30 × 20 cm/12 × 8 inch Swiss roll tins (jelly roll pans), line with greaseproof (waxed) paper, then grease the paper.
2. Put the eggs and sugar in a bowl and whisk with an electric beater until thick and mousse-like. Carefully fold in the flour and hazelnuts with the oil.
3. Turn the mixture into the prepared tins (pans) and level the surface. Bake in a preheated oven (200°C/400°F), Gas Mark 6, for 8 to 10 minutes until the cakes spring back when lightly pressed in the centre.
4. Wring out two clean tea-towels in hot water. Lay them on a work surface, place a sheet of greaseproof (waxed) paper on each and dredge lightly with caster sugar.
5. Turn the sponges upside down on to the paper. Carefully peel off the lining paper and trim off the crisp edges all around the cakes. Turn the bottom edge in neatly for the first roll, then continue to roll with the paper inside. Repeat with the other cake. Place on a wire rack with the joins underneath and leave to cool.
6. To make the filling: whip the cream until it stands in soft peaks. Crush the raspberries lightly with a fork then fold into the cream with the icing (confectioners') sugar. Unroll the sponges and re-move the paper. Divide the filling between the two cakes then roll up again carefully.
7. Before serving, decorate the rolls with cream and raspberries, if using. ·7·11·

C · O · U · N · T · D · O · W · N

The day before:

Make the herb pancakes (crêpes) and spinach pancakes. Make the mushroom and ham filling and the chicken filling. Assemble the pancakes without adding the butter and cheese topping. Cover and refrigerate. If serving a salad, make the dressing and store in a screw-top jar in the refrigerator. Make the hazelnut sponge cakes, rolls and store in an airtight container.

On the day:

Whip the cream and make up the filling for the Raspberry and Hazelnut Roll. Unroll the sponge cakes and divide the filling between them. Re-roll and decorate with cream and raspberries. Refrigerate until required.

To serve at 1 pm:

11.30: Make up any sangria or punch. Set out the table. Arrange the cheeseboard and cover.

12.00: Chill the white wine if using. Prepare the salad ingredients. Blanch the carrots. Assemble the salad without dressing.

12.20: Preheat the oven.

12.30: Melt the butter and brush over the pancakes, then sprinkle with cheese.

12.40: Place the pancakes in the oven.

12.55: Dress the salad if serving. Arrange the dishes on the table.

F · R · E · E · Z · E · R · N · O · T · E · S

Make and cool the pancakes, then wrap, stacked with greaseproof (waxed) paper between each. They can be frozen with the filling, but it is preferable to freeze this separately. Only the ham and mushroom filling is suitable for freezing. The cooked chicken meat can be chopped, wrapped in foil and placed in a polythene (plastic) bag, then frozen. The hazelnut sponge cakes can be frozen at the end of stage 5. Open freeze, then cover with cling film (plastic wrap) and place in polythene bags; seal. Defrost at room temperature, then store in an airtight container.

Cook's Tip:

Instead of folding the pancakes, try making eight larger ones and stacking them with the filling in between. Cover with foil and reheat in the same way. Serve cut in wedges.

Variation:

Try a different mixture of soft summer fruits in the Raspberry and Hazelnut roll. Strawberries with blackcurrants and redcurrants would be a delicious combination.

MENU

· 13 ·

Festive Fare for 8

Celebration Turkey
Buttered Sprouts
Roast Potatoes
Ginger Orange Carrots
·
Christmas Pudding

Christmas is the most important time of year for family entertaining and reunions. It is also a very busy time of year for everyone, so that by the time Christmas Day arrives no one wants to spend most of the time in the kitchen. With this menu there is much that can be prepared in advance, to allow you to spend as much time as possible with family and friends.

Festive Turkey
Celebration Turkey is an excellent dish for busy people as it can be prepared and frozen 2 or 3 weeks before Christmas. A butcher will always bone the turkey if you are unsure about this, but remember to give him plenty of notice during this hectic period! It is essential to use a fresh bird for this dish.

Decorating the Table
There are many ideas for Christmas table settings but red, green, gold and silver in various combinations make the most popular colour themes. Festive paper napkins, crackers, candles and Christmas table decorations all add to the occasion. Serve a light chilled sparkling wine, like an Asti Spumante.

Celebration Turkey

Metric/Imperial	American
1 × 3.5 kg/8 lb oven-ready hen turkey	1 × 8 lb oven-ready hen turkey
salt	salt
freshly ground black pepper	freshly ground black pepper
50 g/2 oz cooked ham	2 slices cooked cured ham
50 g/2 oz fresh breadcrumbs	1 cup fresh bread crumbs
finely grated rind of 1 small lemon	finely grated rind of 1 small lemon
125 g/4 oz fresh spinach, blanched, drained and chopped	½ cup blanched, drained and chopped spinach
750 g/1½ lb boneless turkey meat, minced	3 cups ground turkey meat
40 g/1½ oz butter	3 tablespoons butter
40 g/1½ oz large button mushrooms, trimmed	½ cup trimmed large button mushrooms
flat-leafed parsley, to garnish	flat-leafed parsley, for garnish

1. Bone the turkey, except for the wings and drumsticks. Lay the bird, breast down, on a board. Using a small sharp knife, make a slit down the centre of the back, starting at the neck end. Scrape the flesh away from the rib cage down to the leg and wing joint and cut through the sinews, holding the wings and legs in place. Finally work the flesh away from the breast bone, taking care not to cut through the skin, and remove the carcass.

2. Place the turkey skin down and sprinkle the flesh liberally with salt and pepper. Arrange the ham slices over the turkey flesh.

3. Mix together the breadcrumbs, lemon rind and spinach with salt and pepper to taste. Spread over the ham, then cover with the minced (ground) turkey, stuffing it into the tops of the legs.

4. Melt 15 g/½ oz (1 tablespoon) of the butter in a small pan and gently sauté the mushrooms. Arrange

down the centre of the stuffing and pour the butter and juices on top.

5. Fold up the sides of the turkey to make a compact shape. Sew together, using a trussing needle and string. Turn the bird up the right way.

6. Place on a rack in a roasting tin and spread with the remaining butter. Roast in a preheated oven (160°C/325°F), Gas Mark 3, for 2½ hours or until the juices run clear when the thigh is pierced with a skewer. Baste every 30 minutes.

7. Leave the turkey to stand for about 15 minutes. Meanwhile make the gravy.

8. Carve the turkey crossways into slices. Serve hot, with the gravy. Garnish with flat-leafed parsley.

Buttered Sprouts

Metric/Imperial	American
1.5 kg/3 lb Brussels sprouts	3 lb Brussels sprouts
salt	salt
75 g/3 oz butter	⅓ cup butter
3 tablespoons flaked almonds (optional)	3 tablespoons slivered almonds (optional)
freshly ground black pepper	freshly ground black pepper

1. Trim the sprouts and make a small cross in the base of each one. Cook in a saucepan of boiling salted water for 12 to 14 minutes until just tender. Drain well.

2. Melt the butter in a clean saucepan and add the almonds, if used. Stir in the cooked sprouts and mix gently with the butter and almonds. Add salt and pepper to taste. Transfer to a warm serving dish.

Roast Potatoes

Arrange 1.5 kg/3 lb peeled and parboiled medium potatoes around the turkey, or in a separate roasting tin using some of the turkey fat, for the last 1½ hours of cooking time.

Ginger Orange Carrots

Metric/Imperial	American
1.5 kg/3 lb carrots, sliced	*3 lb carrots, sliced*
75 g/3 oz butter	*1/3 cup butter*
1/2 teaspoon ground ginger	*1/2 teaspoon ground ginger*
salt	*salt*
freshly ground black pepper	*freshly ground black pepper*
450 ml/3/4 pint orange juice	*2 cups orange juice*
3 tablespoons chopped fresh parsley	*3 tablespoons chopped fresh parsley*

Celebration turkey with spinach and mushroom stuffing. Serve hot garnished with Buttered sprouts and flat-leafed parsley.

1. Layer the sliced carrots in a large shallow pan with the butter, ginger, salt and pepper to taste.
2. Pour over the orange juice. Cover and cook very gently for 15 to 20 minutes or until the carrots are just tender. They should still retain some bite. Transfer to a warm serving dish.
3. Sprinkle with chopped parsley and serve immediately.

E·N·T·E·R·T·A·I·N·I·N·G

Christmas Pudding

Metric/Imperial
125 g/4 oz each currants,
  raisins, sultanas and
  mixed peel
175 g/6 oz mixed nuts,
  chopped
125 g/4 oz black treacle
125 g/4 oz fresh wholemeal
  breadcrumbs
125 g/4 oz shredded suet
1 medium carrot, grated
1 eating apple, cored and
  grated
1 teaspoon ground mixed
  spice
125 g/4 oz dark soft brown
  sugar
grated rind of 1 lemon
grated rind of 1/2 orange
2 eggs
8 tablespoons brandy
extra brandy, for flaming

American
3/4 cup each currants,
  raisins, golden raisins,
  and candied peel
1 1/2 cups chopped mixed
  nuts
1/3 cup molasses
2 cups fresh wholewheat
  bread crumbs
3/4 cup shredded suet
1 medium carrot, grated
1 dessert apple, cored and
  grated
1 teaspoon ground mixed
  spice
2/3 cup dark soft brown
  sugar
grated rind of 1 lemon
grated rind of 1/2 orange
2 eggs
8 tablespoons brandy
extra brandy, for flaming

1. Place the dried fruit, peel, nuts, treacle (molasses) breadcrumbs, suet, carrot, apple, spices, sugar and fruit rinds in a large bowl and mix together.
2. Beat the eggs with the brandy and stir into the other ingredients. Mix together thoroughly. Add any silver coins or charms.
3. Spoon the pudding mixture into a greased 1.2 litre/2 pint (5 cup) pudding basin (heatproof mixing bowl). Cover with a double layer of greased greaseproof (waxed) paper pleated down the centre, then enclose in a cloth or a double thickness of foil.
4. Steam the pudding for 8 hours. Remove from the pan of water and allow the pudding to cool.
5. Remove the pudding cloth or foil and paper, and cover the pudding with fresh greased greaseproof paper. Overwrap in foil and store in a cool place.
6. On the day, steam the pudding for a further 2 hours. Turn it out on to a warm plate. Warm some brandy in a spoon or ladle, pour over the pudding and carefully set alight. Serve with brandy butter.

C·O·U·N·T·D·O·W·N

In September/October:
Make the Christmas Pudding. Rewrap well and store.
Two days before:
Thaw the turkey, if necessary. Make brandy butter if required, cover with cling film (plastic wrap) and refrigerate.
On Christmas Eve:
Prepare the Celebration Turkey, cranberry sauce, and stock for the gravy. Prepare the Brussels sprouts. Prepare the carrots.
On Christmas Day:
To serve at 1 pm:
10.00: Preheat the oven.
10.15: Put the turkey in the oven.
11.00: Place the pudding in the steamer. Parboil the potatoes and drain.
11.20: Heat the fat in a roasting pan in the oven.
11.30: Place the potatoes in the roasting pan.
12.30: Drain the carrots and layer in the saucepan. Add the orange juice and cook the carrots.
12.40: Cook the Brussels sprouts.
12.45: Remove the turkey from the oven and allow to stand before carving. Raise the oven temperature to 220°C/425°F, Gas Mark 7, to brown the potatoes.
12.50: Make the gravy.
12.55: Toss the sprouts in butter and almonds. Garnish the carrots before serving.

F·R·E·E·Z·E·R · N·O·T·E·S

Make up the Celebration Turkey, wrap in foil and place in a polythene (plastic) bag; seal and freeze for up to 3 weeks. To thaw, remove the polythene bag and leave at room temperature for 36 to 40 hours. Unwrap and cook as in the recipe.

MENU

· 14 ·

Champagne Celebration for 24

Pork and Sage Terrine
Fresh Salmon Pâté
Melon, Walnut and Avocado Salad
Chicken with Horseradish Cream
Three Cheese Green Salad
Provençal Tomatoes

·

Strawberry and Almond Cheesecake
Fresh Pineapple Centrepiece

A special celebration such as a wedding, important birthday or anniversary calls for an elaborate and impressive feast! This menu should provide just that and with good organization you should be able to do most of the work beforehand.

The Buffet Table
Set the food out on a large table if you have one, or hire two or three trestle tables and put them together. It is better if guests can move around the table and help themselves to each dish. The quantities are quite generous so there should be plenty for everyone!

To set off such an impressive feast, get out your best linen and china. Add a centrepiece of pretty flowers, and light the candles for an evening event. If necessary, fine china can easily be hired with cutlery and glasses.

No grand celebration is complete without 'bubbles', either champagne or sparkling wine such as Asti Spumante. Serve the champagne as it is, or try making Bucks Fizz cocktails.

Pork and Sage Terrine

Metric/Imperial	American
3 bay leaves	3 bay leaves
5 juniper berries or black peppercorns	5 juniper berries or black peppercorns
200 g/7 oz streaky bacon	7 oz bacon slices
350 g/12 oz pig's liver	3/4 lb pork liver
1 small onion	1 small onion
1 clove garlic, peeled	1 clove garlic, peeled
350 g/12 oz pork sausagemeat	3/4 lb pork sausage meat
1 teaspoon chopped fresh sage	1 teaspoon chopped fresh sage
2 hard-boiled eggs, finely chopped	2 hard-cooked eggs, finely chopped
salt	salt
freshly ground black pepper	freshly ground black pepper
350 g/12 oz pork tenderloin	3/4 lb pork tenderloin

1. Lightly grease a 1 kg/2 lb loaf tin, or a terrine of comparable size. Make a pattern on the base with upturned bay leaves and juniper berries or peppercorns.
2. Line the terrine with the bacon. Do not trim any overlapping pieces, as they can be folded over to help keep the filling in place.
3. Mince (grind) together the liver, onion and garlic, then mix well with the sausagemeat, herbs, hard-boiled (hard-cooked) eggs, salt and pepper.
4. Slice the pork tenderloin lengthways into thin strips. Place these strips between two sheets of greaseproof (waxed) paper and beat them with a rolling pin until very thin and tenderized.
5. Place a layer of the liver mixture in the base of the terrine, then cover with pork tenderloin strips. Repeat these layers until the dish is full. Fold over any overlapping bacon.
6. Place the lid on the terrine or, if using a loaf tin, seal well with foil. Cook the terrine in a bain-marie (an ovenproof pan or dish filled with water to come halfway up the sides of the dish) in a preheated oven (180°C/350°F), Gas Mark 4, for 1 1/2 hours.
7. Remove the lid from the terrine, cover with greaseproof paper and place heavy weights or a clean brick on the top to press the terrine into a good shape. Cool, then refrigerate.
8. When ready to serve, uncover and turn out the terrine on to a serving platter. Cut into slices as required. Make two to serve 24. ·13·

Fresh Salmon Pâté

Metric/Imperial	American
750 g/1 1/2 lb fresh salmon or sea trout	1 1/2 lb fresh salmon or sea trout
1 small onion, sliced	1 small onion, sliced
1 carrot, sliced	1 carrot, sliced
2 bay leaves	2 bay leaves
150 ml/1/4 pint white wine	2/3 cup white wine
175 g/6 oz unsalted butter, creamed	3/4 cup unsalted butter, creamed
Sauce:	Sauce:
75 g/3 oz butter	1/3 cup butter
75 g/3 oz plain flour	3/4 cup all-purpose flour
600 ml/1 pint milk	2 1/2 cups milk
2 teaspoons lemon juice	2 teaspoons lemon juice
salt	salt
freshly ground black pepper	freshly ground black pepper
To Garnish:	For Garnish:
1/2 cucumber, cut into thin rings	1/2 cucumber, cut into thin rings
1 hard-boiled egg, yolk sieved, white chopped	1 hard-cooked egg, yolk sieved, white chopped
1 tablespoon chopped fresh parsley	1 tablespoon chopped fresh parsley

1. Place the salmon in a large saucepan and add the onion, carrot, bay leaves and wine. Add just enough water to cover, then bring the fish slowly to the boil. Simmer gently for 15 to 20 minutes. Remove from

the heat and allow the fish to cool in the liquid.

2. Meanwhile make up the sauce base. Melt the butter in a saucepan, remove from the heat and stir in the flour. Cook for 2 to 3 minutes, stirring. Gradually add the milk, beating well between each addition until really smooth. Simmer gently for 3 to 4 minutes, stirring. Add the lemon juice, salt and pepper and allow to cool.

3. Skin and flake the cooked salmon. Pass it through a food processor or pound using a pestle and mortar.

4. When all the ingredients are cool, blend together the fish, sauce and creamed butter. Check and adjust the seasoning and place the pâté in a serving dish. Cover with cling film (plastic wrap) until ready to garnish.

5. Arrange the cucumber round the outside, then the chopped egg white, and finish with the sieved egg yolk and chopped parsley.

Melon, Walnut and Avocado Salad

Metric/Imperial	American
1 honeydew melon	1 honeydew melon
2 avocados	2 avocados
1 lettuce, shredded	1 lettuce, shredded
50 g/2 oz walnut halves, chopped	1/2 cup chopped walnut halves
25 g/1 oz sultanas	3 tablespoons golden raisins
Dressing:	Dressing:
150 ml/1/4 pint olive oil	2/3 cup olive oil
50 ml/2 fl oz red wine vinegar	1/4 cup red wine vinegar
juice of 1/2 lemon	juice of 1/2 lemon
1 teaspoon French whole-seed mustard	1 teaspoon Dijon whole-grain mustard
1 teaspoon sugar	1 teaspoon sugar
1 teaspoon dried dill weed	1 teaspoon dried dill weed
salt	salt
freshly ground black pepper	freshly ground black pepper

1. Cut the melon in half lengthways, remove the seeds and cut out rounds of flesh with a ball cutter. If you do not have such a cutter, dice the melon flesh into 1 cm/1/2 inch cubes.

2. Halve each avocado and discard the stone (pit). Remove the skin and dice the flesh. Add to the melon balls and toss together.

3. Arrange the shredded lettuce in a shallow salad bowl, then spoon over the melon and avocado. Sprinkle the walnuts and sultanas (golden raisins) over the top.

4. To make the dressing, place all the ingredients in a screw-top jar and shake vigorously until well blended. Taste and adjust the seasoning. Pour over the salad, making sure the avocado is completely covered. Serve immediately. ·6·

Chicken with Horseradish Cream

Metric/Imperial	American
2 × 1.5 kg/3 1/2 lb chickens, poached, cooled and shredded	2 × 3 1/2 lb chickens, poached, cooled and shredded
500 g/1 lb waxy potatoes, cooked, peeled and sliced	1 lb waxy potatoes, cooked, peeled and sliced
250 g/8 oz button mushrooms, sliced	2 cups sliced button mushrooms
3 tablespoons chopped fresh parsley	3 tablespoons chopped fresh parsley
3 tablespoons horseradish sauce	3 tablespoons horseradish sauce
600 ml/1 pint mayonnaise	2 1/2 cups mayonnaise
salt	salt
freshly ground black pepper	freshly ground black pepper
To Garnish:	For Garnish:
3 hard-boiled eggs	3 hard-cooked eggs
175 g/6 oz peeled prawns	1 cup shelled shrimp
1 tablespoon chopped fresh parsley	1 tablespoon chopped fresh parsley

1. Place the shredded chicken in a large bowl together with the potato slices, button mushrooms and chopped parsley.
2. Mix the horseradish into the mayonnaise and add salt and pepper.
3. Pour the mixture over the chicken, and toss gently together with the fingertips or two large forks. When well combined, check and adjust the seasoning. Pile the mixture on to a large platter.
4. To garnish the dish, separate the eggs, chop the whites finely and sieve the yolks. Sprinkle the whites over the chicken. Make a pattern over the top of the dish with the sieved yolks, peeled prawns (shelled shrimp) and parsley.

Chicken with horseradish cream; Pork and sage terrine; Fresh pineapple centrepiece; Provençal tomatoes; Three cheese green salad.

Three Cheese Green Salad

Metric/Imperial	American
1 bunch of spring onions, trimmed and sliced lengthways	*1 bunch of scallions, trimmed and sliced lengthwise*
½ cucumber, sliced	*½ cucumber, sliced*
1 lettuce, torn into pieces	*1 lettuce, torn into pieces*
4 small courgettes, cut into matchstick lengths	*4 small zucchini, cut into matchstick lengths*

E·N·T·E·R·T·A·I·N·I·N·G

1 box cress, cut and washed
1 tablespoon chopped chives
Dressing:
125 g/4 oz Stilton cheese
125 g/4 oz full-fat soft
  cheese
75 g/3 oz Camembert
1 tablespoon clear honey
1 tablespoon lemon juice
3 tablespoons olive oil
1 teaspoon Dijon mustard
salt
freshly ground black pepper

1 box garden cress, cut and
  washed
1 tablespoon chopped chives
Dressing:
1/4 lb Stilton cheese
1/2 cup full-fat curd cheese
3 oz Camembert
1 tablespoon runny honey
1 tablespoon lemon juice
3 tablespoons olive oil
1 teaspoon Dijon mustard
salt
freshly ground black pepper

1. Place all the prepared salad ingredients in a large salad bowl.
2. Place all the dressing ingredients in a blender or food processor and blend until well incorporated.
3. Pour the dressing over the salad and toss well.

Provençal Tomatoes

Metric/Imperial
6 continental tomatoes,
  peeled and sliced
1 Spanish onion, cut into
  rings
1 tablespoon chopped fresh
  basil or 1/2 tablespoon
  dried
Dressing:
2 tablespoons olive oil
1 tablespoon white wine
  vinegar
1 teaspoon French mustard
1 clove garlic, peeled and
  crushed
2 teaspoons lemon juice
salt
freshly ground black pepper

American
6 large tomatoes, peeled and
  sliced
1 Spanish onion, cut into
  rings
1 tablespoon chopped fresh
  basil or 1/2 tablespoon
  dried
Dressing:
2 tablespoons olive oil
1 tablespoon white wine
  vinegar
1 teaspoon Dijon-style
  mustard
1 clove garlic, peeled and
  crushed
2 teaspoons lemon juice
salt
freshly ground black pepper

1. Arrange the tomato and onion slices in layers in a shallow dish, sprinkling with a little basil between each layer, and finishing with a layer of onion.
2. To make the dressing, place the ingredients in a screw-top jar and shake really well.
3. Pour the dressing over the salad at least 30 minutes before serving.

Strawberry and Almond Cheesecake

Metric/Imperial
Sponge Base:
50 g/2 oz soft margarine,
  at room temperature
50 g/2 oz self-raising
  flour, sifted
1/2 teaspoon baking powder
1 egg
50 g/2 oz caster sugar
Filling:
350 g/12 oz full-fat soft
  cheese
75 g/3 oz caster sugar
15 g/1/2 oz powdered
  gelatine
3 tablespoons water
1 teaspoon vanilla essence
200 ml/1/3 pint double or
  whipping cream,
  whipped
3 egg whites, stiffly
  whisked
250 g/8 oz strawberries
To Decorate:
1 tablespoon sifted icing
  sugar
85 ml/3 fl oz double or
  whipping cream, stiffly
  whipped

American
Sponge Base:
1/4 cup soft margarine, at
  room temperature
1/2 cup self-rising flour,
  sifted
1/2 teaspoon baking powder
1 egg
1/4 cup sugar
Filling:
3/4 lb full-fat curd cheese
1/3 cup sugar
1 envelope gelatin
3 tablespoons water
1 teaspoon vanilla
7/8 cup heavy or whipping
  cream, whipped
3 egg whites, stiffly
  whisked
1/2 lb strawberries
To Decorate:
1 tablespoon sifted
  confectioners' sugar
6 tablespoons heavy or
  whipping cream, stiffly
  whipped

Strawberry and almond cheesecake.

1. Grease and line an 18 cm/7 inch sandwich tin (layer cake pan). Place the margarine, flour, baking powder, egg and sugar in a bowl and whisk until light and fluffy. Transfer to the prepared tin. Bake in a preheated oven (180°C/350°F), Gas Mark 4, for 20 minutes. Turn out on to a wire rack to cool.

2. To make the filling, mix the cheese with the sugar. Dissolve the gelatine in the water over a gentle heat and add to the cheese with the vanilla essence. Fold in the whipped cream. Lightly fold the whisked egg whites into the cheese mixture.

3. Lightly oil the sides of a 16 cm/6½ inch loose-based cake tin. Cut the sponge in half horizontally and place the bottom half in the tin.

4. Reserving 6 strawberries for decoration, slice the rest on to the sponge base. Pour in the cheesecake mixture and top with the reserved sponge. Chill until set.

5. When set, carefully remove from the tin. Dust the top with sifted icing (confectioners') sugar. Decorate with whirls of cream and the reserved strawberries. Make four to serve 24. ·7·9·10·13·

Fresh Pineapple Centrepiece

1. Choose a very large ripe pineapple with good leaves. The best variety to buy is called a Hass, which is available in May. It has large and attractive leaves, with a wonderful flavour.

2. Cut off the top and base. Discard the base and set the leafy top aside.

3. Stand the pineapple upright and, using a large sharp knife, cut away the skin quite deeply. Remove any of the pitted part of the skin that remains.

4. Turn the pineapple on to its side and slice thinly, then re-form the fruit slices in the order in which they were cut.

5. Stand the pineapple upright on a serving dish and pour a little Kirsch or another liqueur of your choice over the fruit. Replace the top leafy slice. The base of the pineapple may be decorated with fresh fruits such as green grapes or with attractive garden leaves.

C · O · U · N · T · D · O · W · N

Two days before:
Make the Pork and Sage Terrines. Cool, wrap and refrigerate. Make the mayonnaise for the chicken. Cover and refrigerate.

The day before:
Make the Fresh Salmon Pâté. Make the dressing for the Melon, Walnut and Avocado Salad. Prepare the melon. Poach the chicken and shred the flesh. Keep refrigerated. Cook, peel and slice the potatoes.

Boil the eggs. Store in a cool place. Make the dressing for the Three Cheese Green Salad and refrigerate. Prepare the spring onions (scallions), cucumber and courgettes (zucchini). Store in polythene bags in the refrigerator. Make the dressing for the Provençal Tomatoes. Peel the tomatoes and store in the refrigerator. Chop the fresh basil if used. Store in a polythene bag in the refrigerator. Make the Strawberry and Almond Cheesecakes. Do not remove from tins or decorate. Cover and store in the refrigerator.

On the day:

To serve at 1.30 pm:

9.00: Prepare the table.

9.30: Wash the lettuce and cress for the Three Cheese Green Salad. Store in the refrigerator. Complete the Provençal Tomatoes. Cover and store in a cool place. Whip the cream for the cheesecakes. Cover and store in the refrigerator.

10.30: Prepare the fresh pineapple for the centre-piece. Cover and store in a cool place.

11.15: Decorate the cheesecakes. Keep cool. Complete the platters of Pork and Sage Terrine and Chicken with Horseradish Cream. Cover loosely and store in a cool place. Garnish the Fresh Salmon Pâté. Cover and keep refrigerated.

12.30: Chill the champagne.

1.15: Finish the salads. Set out the dishes on the table.

F · R · E · E · Z · E · R · N · O · T · E · S

Make the Pork and Sage Terrines. Cool, wrap and freeze. Thaw overnight in the refrigerator. Make the Fresh Salmon Pâté. Wrap and freeze. Thaw overnight in the refrigerator. Poach the chickens, skin and shred the flesh and freeze covered with the poaching liquid. Thaw overnight in the refrigerator. Use as directed in the recipe. The complete cheese-cakes will not freeze successfully, but the sponge cakes will freeze. Cool completely. Wrap individually. Overwrap and seal. Thaw overnight.

I · N · D · E · X

A·C·K·N·O·W·L·E·D·G·E·M·E·N·T·S

British Chicken Information Service 31; Butter Information Council Ltd 6, 23; Californian Raisin Advisory Board 15; Laurie Evans 47, 60, 62; James Jackson 39; Paul Kemp 35; Vernon Morgan 43; Paul Webster 51; Paul Williams 11, 18, 27, 55.

Jacket photography: Clive Streeter   Illustration: Alan Adler